Nathaniel Hawthorne

From photograph by Mayall, & Co.—the so-called "Motley photograph"

NATHANIEL HAWTHORNE:

Man and Writer

EDWARD WAGENKNECHT

NEW YORK

OXFORD UNIVERSITY PRESS 1961

To Jane & John Adams

OF SAN DIEGO

TO MAKEN HEM A GERLAND OF THE GREVES
WERE IT OF WODEBYNDE OR HAWETHORN LEVES

PREFACE

Many years ago Professor Walter Barnes suggested to me that Hawthorne would be a good subject for a psychograph. I have been a long time getting to him, and now that I have arrived I find myself much amused by the numerous warnings which he sets up. "It is not, I apprehend, a healthy kind of mental occupation," so he makes Coverdale tell us in *The Blithedale Romance*, "to devote ourselves too exclusively to the study of individual men and women." Speaking of the Quaker admirer who, having read *The Scarlet Letter* and *Mosses from an Old Manse*, felt that he knew their author better than his best friend, Hawthorne comments dryly, "But I think he considerably overestimates the extent of his intimacy with me." If you wish to detect any author's "essential traits," he says, you must "look through the whole range of his fictitious characters, good and evil." His son Julian makes the situation even worse so far as his father is concerned when he tells us that Hawthorne "the man and the writer were . . . as different as a mountain from a cloud."

This book is neither a chronological biography nor a critical study, though it contains much information about Hawthorne's life and his works. It is simply a study of Hawthorne's character and personality, based on his writings, his letters and journals, and on all that has been written about him. It uses the methods of Gamaliel Bradford and Sainte-Beuve. It should be judged entirely by reference to the author's success or failure in understanding Nathaniel Hawthorne as a human being and his ability or lack of it to share this understanding with his readers. All other considerations are irrelevant.

Despite its name, psychography has nothing to do with psychoanalysis. Neither is a psychograph an essay, though a few persons imperfectly acquainted with the English language have so described it. It is the very hallmark of the essay that it is tentative, personal, and partial. The psychographer seeks to establish traits and characteristics by the citation of evidence which can be checked by other investigators and which, if he has used his findings properly, can be overthrown only by the citation of fresh evidence. In his investigations and in the presentation of his findings the psychographer is bound by the same laws and standards which govern the chronological biographer, but his organization is different and his aim is more specialized.

I have used the conventional three or four dots to indicate omissions from quoted matter but, inasmuch as I do not pretend to be quoting documents in their entirety, I have not used dots at the beginning or the end of quotations. For appearance sake I have indented the first line of nearly all long quotations set apart from my text.

I pray the ghost of Geoffrey Chaucer to forgive me for changing a pronoun in my quotation from "The Knightes Tale" in order to make it suitable in a dedication addressed to two persons.

Before I had written a line of my book, Hawthorne's great-grandson, Manning Hawthorne, gave me unrestricted permission to quote anything I might wish to use from Hawthorne manuscript material. I am greatly touched by this evidence of his confidence in me, and I cannot too warmly express my gratitude.

My next greatest debt is to Professor Randall Stewart, of Vanderbilt University, whose authority as a Hawthorne scholar is unquestioned. Not only did Professor Stewart give me permission to quote from his editions of Hawthorne's *English* and *American* Notebooks, but he read my entire manuscript and gave me much good advice and encouragement. To him, also, I am very grateful, and I must add that he is in no sense responsible for anything I have written.

Miss Margaret M. Lothrop, present owner and inhabitant of The Wayside, at Concord, Massachusetts, who has made a visit to Hawthorne's old home one of the high spots of their trip to the Boston area for so many Americans, has generously allowed me to use her Hawthorne notes.

Mrs. Margaret Parsons, literary editor of the Worcester (Mass.) *Telegram*, has kindly permitted me to quote from a letter of Louisa May Alcott owned by her.

Mr. Robert Schaffer, of Concord, New Hampshire, whose mother is my first cousin, and his wife Mary have unselfishly labored for me among the Hawthorne letters at the New Hampshire Historical Society.

Professors B. Bernard Cohen of The University of Wichita, Norman Holmes Pearson of Yale University, William M. White of Virginia Polytechnic Institute, and Mrs. Evelyn Johnson Lebacqz of Atherton, California, have permitted me to quote from their respective doctoral dissertations, which are described in my notes.

Houghton Mifflin Company have permitted the use of material from *Hawthorne and His Publisher*, by Caroline Tecknor, which they published in 1913.

I am also grateful for hospitality and permissions to the following libraries and librarians:

The Houghton Library, Harvard University (Dr. William A. Jackson and his assistant, Miss Carolyn Jakeman)

The Berg Collection of The New York Public Library (Dr. John D. Gordan and his staff)

The Pierpont Morgan Library (Mr. Frederick B. Adams, Jr. and his staff)

The Boston Public Library (Mr. Zoltan Haraszti, keeper of rare books, and his staff)

The Essex Institute, Salem (Mrs. Julia Barrow, assistant librarian)

The Massachusetts Historical Society (Mr. Stephen T. Riley and his assistant, Miss Winifred Collins)

The Longfellow House (Mr. Thomas H. de Valcourt, curator)

The New Hampshire Historical Society (Mr. Philip N. Guyol, director; Mrs. Russell B. Tobey, librarian)

EDWARD WAGENKNECHT

Boston University
August 1, 1960

CONTENTS

NATHANIEL HAWTHORNE:
MAN AND WRITER

CHAPTER ONE

A MAN OF OLD SALEM

I

What was he like, this man Hawthorne, whose eyes gaze out upon us so quizzically from the old portraits? His reputation has never been higher than it is today, though many of his admirers seem as alien to his spirit as they are to Cooper or Longfellow or Lowell or any of his other contemporaries whom they neglect. He is admired because he used symbols and produced fiction which can be read upon multiple levels, because he was given to literary ambivalences which suggest the kind of hidden depths into which a psychologically oriented age likes to probe. Are these the significant things about him, or is there something more? And are we, perhaps, in some danger of making him over into our own image?

What sort of man was he? What was his experience of life, and what resources did he bring to this experience? How did he live in the world which all men know and in that other world so intimately but obscurely related to it which only the artist can enter? What did the great nineteenth-century discovery of nature mean to him? How did he come through the special ordeal of his time which centered upon the slavery crisis? What did love mean to him? What relationship did he sustain to his God?

Nathaniel Hathorne (later, by his own fiat, Hawthorne) was born in Salem, Massachusetts, on July 4, 1804, the second

3

of three children of Nathaniel Hathorne (1775-1808) by his wife, Elizabeth Clarke Manning (1780-1849). His elder sister Elizabeth was born in 1802, his younger sister Mary Louisa in 1808.

The Hathornes traced back to an English yeoman family who were supposed to have taken their name from Hawthorn Hill, overlooking Bray, Berks. The earliest direct ancestor of the writer who has been definitely identified is Thomas Hawthorne, of East Oakley in the hundred of Bray, who was born about the time of the discovery of America. During the lifetime of the first William (born about 1543), the preferred spelling came to be Hathorne.[1]

The first Hathorne in the new world was the third William (1607-1681), who came over with his brother John between 1630 and 1633, settling first in Dorchester and later in Salem. Both he and his son, John Hathorne (1641-1717), were involved in the persecution of witches and Quakers, but it was not to him but to the Reverend Nicholas Noyes that Sarah Good addressed the words "You're a liar! I'm no more a witch than you're a wizard! And if you take my life God will give you blood to drink!" Tradition transferred these words to Rebecca Nurse and had them addressed to Hathorne.

Hawthorne's father followed the sea and married the daughter of a neighboring blacksmith. The Mannings had come from England in 1689. Elizabeth's brother Robert operated a profitable stage-coach line between Salem, Marblehead, and Boston and also became noted as a pomologist.

When Captain Nathaniel Hathorne died in 1808 (interestingly enough in Surinam, the scene of one of the earliest English romances, Mrs. Behn's *Oroonoko*), he left his widow an estate of $296.21. She returned, therefore, with her children, to the Manning house. When her son was nine, an accident to his foot reduced him to a condition of semi-invalidism for some three years. But in the summer of 1816 Mrs. Hathorne and her children moved to a house owned by her brother at Raymond, Maine, in a heavily wooded area on Sebago Lake, and here her boy, who had already discovered the joys of reading during his invalidism, spent the better part of three years reveling in the delights of wood and field.

In 1825, through his uncle's generosity, he was graduated from Bowdoin College, after which he returned to Salem and devoted himself to his literary apprenticeship. In 1828 he published anonymously a romance called *Fanshawe*, but he afterwards disliked this book so much that he not only destroyed every copy he could lay his hands on but never even permitted his wife to become aware of its existence. Meanwhile he was contributing stories, essays, and sketches, for little or no money, anonymously or under a variety of pseudonyms, to *The Token*, *The New England Magazine*, *The Democratic Review*, and other periodicals. Most of these were collected in *Twice-Told Tales* (1837, 1842), *Mosses from an Old Manse* (1846), and *The Snow-Image and Other Twice-Told Tales* (1852). With the help of his sister Elizabeth he edited S. G. Goodrich's *American Magazine of Useful and Entertaining Knowledge* for a period in 1836; the same team wrote or compiled the long-popular *Peter Parley's Universal History*, which was published in the same year. *Grandfather's Chair*, stories from early American history retold for children, were published by his future sister-in-law, Elizabeth P. Peabody, the very embodiment of Boston enlightenment and reforming zeal, in 1841-42.

By this time Hawthorne had met and fallen in love with Sophia Peabody, of Salem and Boston, and on July 9, 1842, they were married and went to live in the Old Manse, beside the Revolutionary battlefield at Concord. There their first child Una was born on March 3, 1844, and there, despite their poverty, they were idyllically happy. Poverty had already delayed their marriage and driven Hawthorne to employment in the Boston Custom House from 1839 to 1841, and in 1841, even more surprisingly, to participation in the famous experiment in communal living which George Ripley, George Bradford, and others were conducting at Brook Farm in West Roxbury. He had hoped that Brook Farm would solve his financial problem and make it possible for him to establish a home for Sophia more quickly than he could achieve it in any other way, but this hope was not realized.

In October 1845 the Hawthornes left the Old Manse and returned to Salem, where their only son Julian was born on July 14, 1846. From 1846 to 1849 Hawthorne served in the Salem Custom House, and it was not until the Whigs turned him out that he settled down to write *The Scarlet Letter* (1850). Though this book was produced under the most difficult conditions possible—Hawthorne's mother died during its composition—it ushered in his only great period of fecundity, being followed in 1851 by *The House of the Seven Gables* and in 1852 by *The Blithedale Romance* (which was based upon Brook Farm memories), to say nothing of the two volumes of Greek myths retold—*A Wonder Book* (1851) and *Tanglewood Tales* (1853)—and his campaign *Life of Franklin Pierce* (1852).

Meanwhile, there had been changes in the life of the Hawthornes. From May 1850 until November 1851 they occupied the Little Red House at Lenox, Massachusetts, in the Berkshires, and here their third and last child Rose was born on May 20, 1851. During the winter of 1851-52 they occupied the house of Mrs. Hawthorne's brother-in-law Horace Mann, at West Newton, Massachusetts, where Hawthorne wrote *The Blithedale Romance*. In May 1852 they returned to Concord, having purchased Bronson Alcott's Hillside, which Hawthorne renamed The Wayside.

How much longer Hawthorne's productive period would have lasted if Franklin Pierce had not rewarded him for his campaign biography by appointing him to the lucrative American consulate at Liverpool is anybody's guess. Hawthorne accepted—even sought—the post because, in spite of his now securely established fame, his income was not large enough to enable him to feel confident about the future. The Hawthornes sailed from Boston on July 6, 1853.

Hawthorne resigned his consulate late in the summer of 1857 but did not leave England until January 5, 1858, when, with his family and their new governess Ada Shepard, he left for Paris and Italy. Between November 1858 and the spring of 1859 Una was very ill with Roman fever, which for a time caused her life to be despaired of and which seems permanently to have wrecked her health. In May 1859 the family returned to England, from which they did not return to America until late in June, 1860. *The Marble Faun* (or *Transformation*, as they called it in the English edition) was written in Italy and England in 1859 and published early in 1860; this was the only ripened aesthetic fruit of the European years. *Our Old Home* (1863) was based on Hawthorne's English notebooks; these, like his other notebooks, were published in part by Mrs. Hawthorne, but the complete texts of the English and American notebooks have appeared only in our own time, and we still await the complete text of the French and Italian notebooks.

After returning to Concord, Hawthorne added what he hoped would be an Italianate tower to The Wayside and struggled hard to write an English romance about a bloody footstep, a missing heir, and an American claimant to a great

English estate, but his health was broken and he was not able to achieve his aim. "The Ancestral Footstep" he had abandoned in England when the idea for *The Marble Faun* came to him. *Septimius Felton*, which has a Concord-Revolutionary War setting, and in which the other themes are less important than the search for an elixir of life, was afterwards edited by Una Hawthorne with assistance from Robert Browning, and *Dr. Grimshawe's Secret* was published as Julian Hawthorne arranged it.[2] As far as it goes, "The Dolliver Romance" is generally considered a more successful treatment of recalcitrant materials than its predecessors, but only three fragments of this work had been written when death came.

After the outbreak of the Civil War, in the spring of 1861, Hawthorne was painfully conscious of the estrangement from his friends in patriotic Concord which his inability to take up their attitude toward the conflict induced. Month after month his health grew worse. In the spring of 1864 he was sent off for a trip under the care of his publisher, William D. Ticknor, but Ticknor died very suddenly in Philadelphia. Hawthorne got back to Concord more dead than alive, only to start off again for the White Mountains with Franklin Pierce. During the night of May 18-19 he died in his sleep at a hotel in Plymouth, New Hampshire.

After Hawthorne's death Mrs. Hawthorne edited his notebooks, as has already been indicated. After a very unhappy quarrel with the publisher James T. Fields over Hawthorne royalties,[3] she left Concord in October 1868 and moved with her children to Dresden. In 1870 they came to London, where Mrs. Hawthorne died in February 1871. Una Hawthorne died in 1877 at the age of thirty-three. Julian, author, businessman, and father of many children, lived until 1933. After the end of her unhappy marriage to George Parsons Lathrop, Rose, who had become a devout Catholic, made a golden name for herself as the guiding saint and presiding genius of homes for cancer patients in New York City and at Hawthorne, New York. She died in 1928.[4]

II

In Liverpool in 1857 Hawthorne had occasion to describe his own appearance: "age (I am sorry to say), fifty-one;—height, five feet, ten and a half inches;—hair dark and somewhat bald;—face, oval; nose straight;—chin, round."

But he was not always fifty-one, and his adoring wife is not the only one who gives us more highly colored portraits of him. Both Elizabeth Peabody and Frank Sanborn thought him handsomer than Byron. To Sophia Ripley at Brook Farm he was "our prince." Rebecca Harding Davis found a "mysterious power" in his face never matched elsewhere "in picture, statue, or human being." Once, taking advantage of her years, an old woman stopped him in the road and requested to be informed whether she was addressing a man or an angel.

Such impressions were not peculiar to women. Frank Stearns thought his features "not only classic but grandly classic"; James T. Fields praised his princely bearing, grand eyes, and melodious voice. To Emerson he was "regal," and Anthony Trollope thought him the handsomest of all Yankees. Augustine Birrell remembered him through a lifetime as the handsomest author he had ever seen, and James Freeman Clarke, who had never laid eyes on him until he was called in to marry him and Sophia, was so impressed by his appearance as to lose a share of his ministerial aplomb.

The eyes were the most impressive feature—"the most magnificent eye," said Charles Reade, "that I ever saw in a human head." Bayard Taylor added that Hawthorne's were the only eyes he had ever seen flash fire. Moncure D. Conway gave them a "*beauté du diable*," and Edward Dicey says they were

" '*distrait*'-looking." Mrs. Fields found them "soft and kind, but in-seeing. I do not remember," she adds, "ever having the impression of being looked at by Hawthorne. There was, how-ever, a very keen sense of one's being understood by him."

There were dissenters, however. S. G. Goodrich describes him coldly in his youth as "of a rather sturdy form, his hair dark and bushy, his eyes steel-gray, his brow thick, his mouth sarcastic, his complexion stony, his whole aspect cold, moody, distrustful." In 1862 Henry James, Sr., saw him at the Satur-day Club and judged him not "a handsome man, nor an engag-ing one personally. He has the look of a rogue who suddenly finds himself in a company of detectives."

Even some women could look at him without getting star-dust in their eyes, Maria Mitchell for one, who had seen plenty of stars in heaven. Yet though he was "not handsome," Miss Mitchell thought he looked "as the author of his books should look; a little strange and odd, as if not of this earth. He has large, bluish-gray eyes; his hair stands out on each side, so much so that one's thoughts naturally turn to combs and hair-brushes and toilet ceremonies as one looks at him."

He was younger when Fredrika Bremer saw him at Lenox, but she too attempted careful discrimination between good points and bad, finding a "bitter expression" in his smile. "The whole upper part of the countenance is classically beautiful, but the lower part does not perfectly correspond and lacks decision of character." He found it impossible to understand her Scandinavian English, and this, added to his natural dif-fidence with strangers, induced, as Miss Bremer herself ex-pressed it, "nossing but seelence" between them. Years later, when he met her again in Rome, Hawthorne good-humoredly looked back to the time when she "went away so dissatisfied with my conversational performances, and so laudatory of my brow and eyes, while so severely criticising my poor mouth and chin." He added, "God bless her good heart! and every inch of her little body, not forgetting her red nose, preposterously big as it is in proportion to the rest of her! She is a most amiable little woman, worthy to be the maiden aunt of the whole human race."

Miss Bremer was not alone, however, in differentiating between the upper and lower halves of Hawthorne's face. Thus Conway found his "massive brow and fine aquiline nose . . . of such commanding strength as to make the mouth and chin seem a little weak by contrast." He adds that the head was shapely in front but flat in the back. Julian says that the brow came to seem more massive as the hair line receded and that the forehead "was hollowed at the temple and rounded out above, after the Moorish style of architecture." He also records that "the straight, rather salient nose had a perceptible cleft at the tip." But whether the mouth indicated weakness or merely sensitiveness seems to have been a matter of taste and judgment; when Longfellow encountered Una after her father's death, he was impressed by her beautiful smile "that flashes all over her face, just as her father's did." All in all, veiled strength, not weakness, seems to have been the dominant impression Hawthorne made. He was "tall, firm, and strong in bearing" (in Thomas Wentworth Higginson's phrase); only Thoreau, upon his first contact, seems to have found him "rather puny-looking" and "one of the not-bad." Lowell thought he looked like a hawk, and when he returned from Europe with the moustache he had raised in Rome, Fields nicknamed him "Field-Marshal Hawthorne." Even in Tom Appleton's famous phrase, "a boned pirate," suggested perhaps by Hawthorne's habit of holding his head slightly on one side, there is no question where the emphasis falls.

III

Through most of his life Hawthorne was an exceptionally healthy man. "We all have colds now, except Mr. Hawthorne, with whom earth's maladies have nothing to do." He did not mind hot weather; he never had a headache; and he himself says he never knew he had bowels or lungs until he came to Rome. When he went back to Bowdoin in 1852 for a class reunion, he was impressed by the snow on the heads of his classmates, but he himself felt almost as young as the day he had graduated.

It was Mrs. Hawthorne's view that her husband was never "obtusely well—he has no brute force; but every part of his frame seems to be in perfect diapason, like a bird's." But there seems to have been no real deficiency of "brute force." When need arose, Hawthorne could shovel snow and saw and split wood without weariness. His hands were large and powerful, and he was skillful with tools. He was an accomplished walker, and he could leap as high as his own shoulder from a standing position.

He did not greatly abuse his health; neither was he unduly careful of it. He shied from English dirt and was afraid of catching a disease in the streets of Liverpool, but this was more fastidiousness than hypochondria. He was also of the opinion that Englishmen overate in comparison with Americans, and at one time during his stay in England he feared that he himself was "getting a little too John Bullish" in his eating and drinking habits, though he adds that he has never felt better.

Of course he was mortal, and therefore he could not always be well. His dismissal from the Salem Custom House, followed by the strain of his mother's death while he was writing *The Scarlet Letter* immediately afterwards, took its toll of him. It was his own feeling that his health suffered in Lenox, and that he became more subject to colds than formerly, but since he had always believed he could not be at his best away from the seacoast this may have been "psychosomatic." All in all, there seems to have been no real break in his health until after the long agony of Una's nearly fatal illness in Rome.

Energy was another matter. Hawthorne is often thought to have had a sluggish temperament. Certainly he had a splendid capacity for indolence in his youth—often a characteristic of massive, slow-growing natures. During the years of his literary apprenticeship, his Salem neighbors considered him a selfish idler living on his mother, but this was partly because they did not know what was going on. "My brother is never idle," Elizabeth Hawthorne told one inquirer austerely. Yet Hawthorne himself declares that he was often apathetic when something he had long desired was placed at last within his reach, and we shall never know whether his disinclination to interfere with other people or with the trend of the times, lest he should do more harm than good, was more the result or the cause of a temperamental bias. Once he amusingly suggested a kind of Rip Van Winkle solution for human problems—"an age-long nap." And Henry Bamford Parkes has interestingly suggested that Hawthorne lived more successfully than either Poe or Melville "chiefly because he was a man of low emotional pressure who made few demands." [5]

But it will not do to overstress this line of reasoning. "I hate all labor," says Hawthorne, "but less that of the hands than of the head." It is hard to believe that the man who created all the enchanting, imaginative toys for his children that Hawthorne made, who amused himself and them by asking them to close their eyes for a moment so that, when they opened them again, they would find him high over their heads in the branches of a neighboring tree, and who once absent-mindedly whittled away the whole leaf of a table while he was thinking—it is difficult to believe that such a man was altogether sluggish.

This is a glorious day [he tells his journal in 1843]. . . . It is good to be alive now. Thank God for breath—yes, for mere breath! —when it is made up of such a heavenly breeze as this. It comes to the cheek with a real kiss; it would linger fondly around us, if it might, but since it must be gone, it caresses us with its whole kindly heart, and passes onward, to caress likewise the next thing that it meets. There is a pervading blessing diffused all over the world. I look out of the window, and think—"Oh perfect day! Oh beautiful world! Oh good God!" And such a day is the promise of a bliss-ful Eternity; our Creator would never have made such weather, and have given us the deep hearts to enjoy it above and beyond all thought, if He had not meant us to be immortal. It opens the gates of Heaven, and gives us glimpses far inward.

This harmonizes with the rhapsody on the joys of living in "The Hall of Fantasy" and with Margaret Fuller's testimony that Hawthorne once told her in Old Manse days that he found this earth so beautiful that he never wished to leave it.

But if Hawthorne's temperament was as healthy as this, what are we to do with the testimony of such persons as Rebecca Manning, who tell us that wherever he went "he carried twilight with him"? To begin with, it should be noted that this is not at all the view of his wife and children. Mrs. Hawthorne called him "our sunshine" and "the light of his home." Rose found him "radiant." She writes, "If he said a few kind words to me, my father gave me a sense of having a strong ally among the great ones of life; and if I were ill, I was roused by his standing beside me to defy the illness." Una and Julian agreed that there was no smile like papa's, and Una, grown-up, said, "He was capable of being the very gayest person I ever saw. He was like a boy. Never was such a play-mate as he in all the world."

Perhaps this is why Julian always felt that his father's books had been written by a different man than the man he remembered. Since an artist lives in his work at least as profoundly as in his day-by-day experiences, it is difficult to follow him all the way here. Yet Hawthorne himself would quite likely have agreed with his son, for he was always greatly distressed by what seemed to him the uncharacteristically gloomy tone of his writings; this is at least one reason why he preferred *The House of the Seven Gables* to *The Scarlet Letter*. He once told Elizabeth Peabody that he had burned some powerful stories because he thought them morbid and unhealthy and that he wished he had burned more. It may be, as F. O. Matthiessen suggests, that his "profoundly Gothic" writer's imagination found beauty only in shadows, and that "an extraordinary number of the central scenes of his novels are enacted under the moon," but he always wanted his wife and children dressed in gay colors. "The sunshine," he said, "can scarcely be too much or too intense for my taste." To be sure, he thought his wife had more natural sunshine in her disposition than he had. And she herself was willing to admit that her husband was "pensive" though not "gloomy." "He always seemed to me, in his remote moods, like a stray Seraph, who had experienced in his own life no evil, but by the intention of a divine intellect, saw and sorrowed over all evil." Once, in England, she even wrote, "I think that for once, at least, Mr. Hawthorne was satisfied with weather and circumstances."

Was Hawthorne, then, an "optimist" or a "pessimist"? Actually he was neither, for the excellent reason that both terms apply to abstractions rather than to human beings. If there are any consistent optimists among the children of men, they must all be cheerful idiots, and if there ever were any consistent pessimists they all committed suicide long ago. Once during Hawthorne's early life, his friend Horatio Bridge thought him in danger of suicide; whether he was right or wrong we shall probably never know.

As I shall show elsewhere, Hawthorne never doubted the Christian view of either the limitations or the capacities of human nature. "Life is made up of marble and mud," he said, and again: "Mankind are earthen jugs with spirits in them." "I have been a happy man," he once wrote R. H. Stoddard, "yet I do not remember any one moment of such happy conspiring circumstances that I could have rung a joy-bell at it." "The Lily's Quest" makes the valid point that "there is no place on earth fit for the site of a pleasure-house because there is no spot that may not have been saddened by human grief, stained by crime, or hallowed by death." But this is not presented as an incitement to despair, and Hawthorne cuts considerably deeper in an idea for a story in which the human heart should be allegorized as a cavern; "the gloom and terror may lie deep," he says, "but deeper still is this eternal beauty."

"The aromatic odor of peat-smoke, in the sunny autumnal air, is very pleasant." Such is one entry in Hawthorne's journal. Henry James would seem to have lacked his usual penetration when he patronizingly remarked that "the reader says to himself that when a man turned thirty gives a place in his mind —and his inkstand—to such trifles as these, it is because nothing else of superior importance demands admission." Hawthorne himself says that what pleased him in his gloomy subjects was "their picturesqueness, their rich duskiness of color, their chiaroscuro." I am sure that the appeal went deeper than "shadowy fancies and conceits" or chiaroscuro, but I do not find that it conduced to hopelessness or despair. The strange thing is that James apparently failed to perceive that without his ability to find pleasure in "the aromatic odor of peat-smoke, in the sunny autumnal air"—or what it symbolizes—Hawthorne would have lacked one very important anchor, or refuge against despair. Willa Cather, who found her own anchors not in ideas but in "merely pictures, vivid memories," would have understood this, and so would Virginia Woolf, who once wrote: "For, Heaven knows why, just as we have lost faith in human intercourse some random collocation of barns and trees or a haystack and a waggon presents us with so perfect a symbol of what is unattainable that we begin the search again."

The reader may possibly feel at this point that the writer has both admitted and denied certain allegations about Hawthorne's temperament. This is very close to what he wished to do. "To his contemporaries in a period characterized by philosophies of freedom that tended toward voluntarism," writes Hyatt H. Waggoner, "he seemed a fatalist; to mechanists of the recent past he seemed old-fashioned in his belief in man's moral responsibility." Hawthorne was no extremist. He stood poised between past and present, the dream and the reality, sense and soul, heart and mind. "My father," says Julian, "was two men, one sympathetic and intuitional, the other critical and logical; together they formed a combination that could not be thrown off its feet." As hard-headed as Solon Shingle he had the faith of the child in the Gospels.

Along this same line it is interesting to note that Emerson, Longfellow, Lowell, Alcott, and George William Curtis all felt that there was a strong feminine element in Hawthorne. Longfellow said that when he was in the room one always spoke as if in the presence of a woman. Lowell put his impression into *A Fable for Critics*:

> When Nature was shaping him, clay was not granted
> For making so full-sized a man as she wanted,
> So, to fill out her model, a little she spared
> From some finer-grained stuff for a woman prepared,
> And she could not have hit a more excellent plan
> For making him fully and perfectly man.

When Margaret Fuller heard of Sophia's engagement to Hawthorne, she wrote perceptively: "I think there will be great
happiness; for if ever I saw a man who combined delicate
tenderness to understand the heart of a woman, with quiet
depth and manliness enough to satisfy her, it is Mr. Hawthorne."

Of course none of these persons intended any suggestion
that Hawthorne was a "womanish" kind of man. How impressive is Julian's story of the day he and his father were caught
in a serious boat accident on the River Mersey:

There came a sudden violent jar and stop, followed by outcries
and shrieks. I looked at my father for my cue: his countenance was
serene, and when a young fellow came headlong down the com-
panionway and seized one of the iron pillars which upheld the deck
overhead, an expression of quiet amusement flickered at his mouth.
. . . Was it fatalism or trust in God? I have often thought it over
since then. To let me be frightened could only have made bad
worse. Death was perhaps a minute away, but he chose to sit still.[6]

Hawthorne well knew that his "native propensities were
toward Fairy Land." He found the picture more enchanting
than the reality, the scene in the mirror more enticing than
that which it reflected. He disliked having great men portrayed realistically. He even enjoyed places more when they
had been "etherealized by distance." Yet he had perfect confidence that a man of letters could do anything that a man of
affairs might do if only he would take the trouble, as Burns
and Chaucer did. Simply because he had so much use as he
did of imagination and sensibility, he was, in his own words,
"rigidly tenacious of what was reasonable in the affairs of real
life." And he had no sympathy with those who rejected the
duties and satisfactions of the common way out of an impossible devotion to a grandiose ideal that was never meant to be
realized upon this earth.[7] As Richard Harter Fogle has well

observed, it is his moderation, his fairness, and his avoidance of extremes—his ability to state fairly even the case which he cannot accept—which have made it possible for some otherwise acute readers completely to misunderstand what he is saying even in such major works as *The Scarlet Letter* and *The Marble Faun*.

IV

Hawthorne was considerably less well equipped for life materially than spiritually. "At one epoch," writes Julian, "the title-deeds to the great estate now the town of Raymond belonged to the Hawthornes; and had they not afterwards been lost, the family would have been one of the wealthiest in New England." But they were lost, and in the increasingly plutocratic Salem in which the Hawthorne children lived only laborers and domestic servants looked up to them. These facts had to be accepted, but resentment was mingled with acceptance. As a small boy, Hawthorne is reported to have had sufficient strength of character to refuse a ten-dollar bill which Uncle Simon Forrester offered him in the street, feeling that Forrester was not closely enough related to patronize him in this way.

Horatio Bridge is certainly gilding the lily when he writes that Robert Manning supplied Hawthorne at college with means as lavish as those of any of his companions. Manning may have done everything he could or should have done; the fact remains that his nephew often found himself almost literally penniless in Brunswick. But his pride was not dead. Once he declared that he could hardly endure his dependence, and once he casually and somewhat cavalierly informed his benefactor that it was "absolutely necessary" he should be as well dressed as his "chum."

His voluntary incarceration of himself in the chamber under

the eaves on Union Street after his graduation was not calcu-
lated to improve his financial condition; neither was it quite
what might have been expected of a canny Yankee. Even when
he sold a story or found employment he was not always paid.
After he had got out his first number of *The American Magazine* in Boston, his stock of ready money was down to thirty-
four cents. "For the Devil's sake," he wrote Louisa, "if you
have money, send me a little. It is now a month since I left
Salem, and not a damned cent have I had, except five dollars
that I borrowed of Uncle Robert—and out of that I paid my
stage fare and other expenses."

It was not much better after he was married. He was very
angry when a story went the rounds that he and Sophia were
starving at the Old Manse, but the story was not far from the
truth; without the river and the garden and the Old Manse
orchards they might well have starved. When Sophia proposed
celebrating Christmas with "a fine bowl of chocolate," he
countered with the suggestion that they do no cooking at all;
so they sat down to a Christmas dinner of preserved fruits,
bread, and milk. Once, when Sophia was away, he made a habit
of going to bed at dusk to save the oil in the lamp.

After *The Scarlet Letter* it was better, yet not startlingly so,
for though *The Scarlet Letter* was, by mid-century standards,
a best seller, it earned Hawthorne only $450 during its first
two years of life. In 1851, nevertheless, his total receipts from
Ticknor and Fields were $1430, and though he never had any
money for life insurance, he playfully told Ticknor, three
years later, that he now considered himself one of the moneyed
men of Massachusetts, having $3000 in investments.

Hawthorne disliked the expanding materialism of his America as much as the Transcendentalists did, and he felt the full
force of the New Testament position that the love of money
is the root of all evil. But there was no cant in his attitude

toward money. Even in the childish "Spectator," though admitting all its corruptions, he declares that it is also "the foundation of almost everything great and good." He did not enjoy the feeling Thoreau gave him that it was disgraceful to have a house to live in or two coats to wear, and it is quite clear that Phoebe, not Holgrave, is his spokesman in *The House of the Seven Gables:* in this short life "one would like a house and a moderate garden-spot of one's own."

What he really would have liked as an adult was a small regular income which should neither diminish nor increase. If it increased he would get his attention fixed on the money itself, and he did not want that. Once he expressed the matter somewhat differently by telling his wife that he would like to have enough money so that he might always find in his pocket whatever anybody might ask him for. The unworldly man who is not a fool is perfectly exemplified in these aspirations. Because he is in the body the money must be there when he needs it, but it must never obtrude itself upon his attention, for it is not interesting in itself.

So far as his relations with Ticknor and Fields were concerned, Hawthorne conducted the business side of his literary life like a babe in the woods. He never knew how much his books had earned or were earning. The publishers acted as his bankers, paying his bills for him upon request and honoring all his demands but making no seasonal remittances and never rendering an account. He did not even dare to buy some books before leaving England without first writing them to inquire whether he could afford it. "If ever I can repay you for all this trouble," he once wrote Ticknor, "by taking charge of your business, you may command me; but I doubt whether you would be quite as well satisfied with my administration as I am with yours."

Yet he was not indifferent to the rewards of authorship.

When Griswold approached him in 1843, he immediately
indicated his willingness to enter into an exclusive agreement
if he could make more money that way. He even considered
writing exclusively for children, and would have considered
it more carefully, he said, if Jacob Abbott and a few others
had not already swept up most of the potential winnings. Even
format was eyed cannily:

If *The Scarlet Letter* is to be the title, would it not be well to
print it on the title-page in red ink? I am not quite sure about the
good taste of so doing, but it would certainly be piquant and appropriate, and, I think, attractive to the great gull whom we are
endeavoring to circumvent.

He was also prepared to use all legitimate means to collect
the money he felt was due him, though, like most sensitive
men, he felt rather mean when he did this. In 1844, authorizing
his friend George Hillard to put the screws on one debtor,
he wrote, "It strikes me as hardly fair, that a debtor should
keep a horse for his private pleasure (as our friend sees fits
to do,) while the creditor trudges about with a hole in his
cowhide boots—as will be my own case, when I take this letter
to the post office." He also used legal means to recover money
he thought due him from Ripley and Dana of Brook Farm,
and won his suit, though he may never actually have collected
on it.[8]

For all Hawthorne's coy, ladylike protestations about his
unwillingness to accept a favor at Pierce's hands, it is clear
that he wanted the Liverpool consulship and went zealously to
work—or put his friends zealously to work—to secure it. While
he held it he squeezed every penny he could out of it, as
indeed he would have been a fool not to do, for he had set
literature aside for some of the best years of his life to acquire
it, and should he fail to acquire a competence through it, the
whole experience must be reckoned a total loss. When "those

jackasses in Washington" threatened to reduce his income, he was furious. Laurence Hall, who has a somewhat quixotic approach to this matter, exaggerates the difference between Hawthorne's earlier and later attitude toward material advancement, but he has shown [9] that Hawthorne was capable of planning (though not perhaps of executing) some pretty sharp, almost questionable maneuvers in his attempt to avoid the threatened calamity. "There is a pleasure in getting around such a mean old scoundrel as Uncle Sam."

Again and again he was tempted to resign the uncongenial office, but he could not make up his mind to do so while there was still money to be made; he hoped the question might be settled for him by his being pushed out. He might have gone to Lisbon as *chargé-d'affaires,* which he knew he ought not to do because of the language difficulties. "I hope Pierce will not offer it, for I cannot answer for myself that I shall do what really seems to me the wisest thing—this is, refuse it." It is amusing to find a frugal mid-nineteenth century Yankee accepting a style of living to which, as the saying goes, he hopes to become accustomed as shamelessly as we do it today:

I do not see how it will be possible for me to live, hereafter, on less than the interest of $40,000. I can't imagine how I ever did live on much less than that. It takes at least $100,000 to make a man quite comfortable . . . and even then he would have to deny himself a great many very desirable things. To sum up the matter, I shall try to be content with a little, but would far rather have a great deal.

And then the old New England frugality—and the New England conscience—make themselves heard again: "I sometimes doubt whether this European residence will be good for us, in the long run. All of us will come back with altered habits, accustomed to many things which we shall not find at home."

But how frugal was Hawthorne? Less so, Ada Shepard thought, than his wife, though he once drove her nearly frantic by insisting on untying an eagerly awaited package because "it was such a very nice cord he must not cut it!" He did not come out of Europe with $100,000, nor $40,000 either. He came out with $30,000, and then lent John O'Sullivan $10,000 which was never returned. There would have been more if the Hawthornes had not lived and traveled on the continent after he gave up his consulship, and above all if he had been able to resist the temptation to give his money away.

He always seemed to want the best accommodations in traveling. In general he loathed petty economies. "Human life," he said, "gets cold and meagre, under such a system." Once he spent £20 on a dinner given in honor of his English friend Francis Bennoch.

When Oscar Wilde, on his arrival in America, was asked whether he had anything to declare, he is said to have replied "Nothing except my genius." In considering Hawthorne's equipment for the battle of life, we have hitherto concerned ourselves with almost everything except his genius. It is time, now, to turn to his most important attribute.

CHAPTER TWO

LEARNING AND DOING

I

A writer practices an art and thus establishes a kinship with all artists. No doubt he is closer to other writers than he is to painters or musicians, but in many important aspects the aesthetic process is the same for every art, and if a writer has any understanding beyond his own particular field one would certainly expect his work to be affected by it.

But the writer's particular art deals outstandingly with ideas as well as emotions. His learning, his principles, his convictions in every area and avenue of experience are involved in it. The consideration of Hawthorne's "genius" as an element in his living may therefore turn out to be a rather more complicated matter than might have been expected.

According to Hawthorne himself he did not like to go to school and avoided it whenever he could. Nevertheless he had a fairly wide experience of schools, and the only time he seems to have been a problem child was at Stroudwater in the autumn of 1818, when Uncle Richard found him so miserable, un-co-operative, and apparently disliked that he did not send him back after Christmas. He tutored for college with a Salem lawyer Benjamin L. Oliver, who did such an excellent job that the boy was ready a year before Uncle Robert wanted him to go.

He was not a model student in college either, yet Professor

Newman praised his compositions highly, and Professor Packard was equally enthusiastic about his Latin. Many years afterwards, Longfellow told George Lathrop he had never forgotten Hawthorne's fine translations. Mathematics, metaphysics, and above all declamation he simply disliked, and until his senior year he seems simply to have refused to apply himself to them.

His Latin was undoubtedly his principal scholastic achievement, and he showed his own sense of this by himself teaching it—along with a little Greek—to his son. He seems to have been rather comfortably at home with French, and he had some familiarity with Spanish and Italian. German he flirted with when it was popular with his Transcendental neighbors, but he did not get far. "He said he wished he could read German," said Mrs. Hawthorne, "but could not take the trouble."

His conservatism in matters of language is well brought out in an 1861 letter to one of his old teachers, Joseph Worcester, thanking him for his dictionary:

Of all Lexicographers, you seem to me best to combine a sense of the *sacredness* of language with a recognition of the changes which time and human vicissitude inevitably work upon it. It will be ominous of anarchy in matters moral and political, when our Dictionaries cease to be mainly conservative; and for my own part, I would not adopt a single new spelling, unless it were forced upon me by the general practice of the age and country;—nor willingly admit a new word, unless it brought a new meaning along with it.

Hawthorne's own adherence to eighteenth-century formality is quite in line with the sentiments expressed here. He had no acquaintance with what we now call literary scholarship, and he seems rather disposed to accept uncritically what people tell him, as, for example, when he records in his *English Notebooks* the gossip about Shakespeare and Davenant.

Science was both more and less important to Hawthorne

than language study, but its importance was almost wholly connected with its capacity to stimulate his imagination. If such early papers as "Footprints on the Sand" tempt us to feel that we see a potential field naturalist in the making, it soon appears that he is really using the specimens over which he muses as a means of feeling his way imaginatively into the life of nature. His closest approach to a scientific paper is the essay on the "Nature of Sleep," but here again what interests him is human consciousness, and he ends by promising his readers that Eternity will "make up" to them for the time they lose in sleep while they are in the flesh.

In the great scientific discoveries and speculations of the nineteenth century, Hawthorne had no more interest than Dickens, and I think Louis Agassiz, whom he, of course, knew personally, is the only contemporary scientist whose name appears in Hawthorne's published writings; he was much more likely to speak of Friar Bacon, Albertus Magnus, or Paracelsus.[1]

Since both Parker Cleaveland and William Smythe were members of the Bowdoin faculty while Hawthorne was a student there, he had for a boy of his time a good exposure to both science and mathematics. But he gave no indication of interest in either professor, nor did he earn good grades in their division of the curriculum. During his senior year, however, he bought a ticket for a series of medical lectures and dissections not a regular part of the curriculum and attended them for three months.

A reasonable number of scientific books appear in his own reading lists, and the number of scientific items he printed in *The American Magazine* while he was in charge, though smaller than under his predecessor, was not inconsiderable. But some of these items attracted him as curiosa and others by their spiritual suggestiveness. Sometimes he is frankly credulous.

In his own writings science plays a smaller role, but the principles of attraction and selection remain unchanged. In the light of the knowledge available in his time, Hawthorne may well have supposed his account of the pre-natal influences brought to bear on Hester's Pearl more "scientific" than it seems to us, but Pearl is still largely an allegorical figure, and science serves the needs of allegory in his portrait of her.

The truth is that Hawthorne did not really trust scientists nor the scientific type of mind, and it was not only because he sought Gothic thrills that he habitually tended to associate scientists with the black arts. If he did not really believe that there is a strain of diabolism in scientists, he did see them as sympathetic toward infidelity, for he knew that even when the scientist is himself a believer, he is necessarily preoccupied with materialities, with the temporal and secular side of man's nature and not with man in his sacred or eternal aspects.

He goes farther still. In his heart of hearts he thought science hostile to the highest human values. He discerned a species of fanaticism in scientists. The scientist's concern with the general rather than the specific, with the race rather than the individual —all this tended to alienate Hawthorne. Once he permits himself to speak of "the murder of a mouse in an air-pump." But as he saw it, scientists did not stop with murdering mice. They murdered themselves and those nearest and dearest to them. Chillingworth is not a fair test case, for Chillingworth is a wronged man who has been warped out of a normal course of development by his wife's infidelity and his own self-dedication to a hideous revenge. But what excuse is to be found for Rappaccini, who, quite without provocation—and without malice—performs a hideous experiment upon his own daughter?

Above all other scientists, the physician is dedicated to the nurture and preservation of life, but Hawthorne's physicians are not, in general, admiringly portrayed. When they are not malevolent, they are eccentric, like Dr. Grimshawe, whose grotesque affection for spiders recalls his creator's long-lived interest in Swift. Only Dr. Dolliver, at the very end of Hawthorne's career, is a quite sympathetic figure.

He does not seem to have believed that doctors, for all their professed devotion, really lost any sleep over the patients they killed. In this aspect he was fairly consistent in electing to do his own dying without medical assistance.

The one scientific theme in which Hawthorne does appear to have been interested is genetics. This appears outstandingly in *The House of the Seven Gables,* which, as Roy R. Male has remarked, is written from an "essentially genetic point of view." Nor is Hawthorne evasive, though he is more than a little subtle, in presenting the sexual implications of his theme, with "the famous Pyncheon bull" serving as an effective symbol. No doubt his interest in genetics was fostered and developed by the fact that he himself was a family man and one more than ordinarily aware of the traits which his own ancestors had passed on to him for good or for ill. Furthermore, he keeps his focus steadily upon human conduct and the human problem, showing no interest in scientific speculation or experimentation as such.[2]

II

From boyhood Hawthorne was a slave to print. Like most bookish people he often saw life itself in terms of literature. "The poor old fellow's story seemed to me almost as worthy of being chanted in immortal song as that of Odysseus or Evangeline," he writes. He once saw a couple at a banquet in terms of Bluebeard and his wife. And when he came to their haunts in England the characters in eighteenth-century novels seemed as real to him as Dr. Johnson himself.

Horatio Bridge says that Hawthorne often quoted scraps of verse in his conversation, and according to Fields he could work up impromptu a whole tissue of literary allusions. Yet he did not quote much in his writings and does not seem to have approved of quotation. Even when Elizabeth was working with him on *The American Magazine*, he urged her not to quote but to put other people's thoughts into her own words and "amalgamate the whole into a mass." He did not own many books; when he moved into The Wayside he himself was dismayed by his gaping shelves, and Howells judged his private collection both paltry and ill-kept. For all that he seems to have had a warm feeling for books. Perhaps it was only his poverty in early life that prevented him from buying books regularly.

In his youth people said of him, as they have said of others, that he had read all the books in the local library. It was not true of course, but this is not the kind of thing that is said about people who do not read extensively. "Hawthorne was a hearty devourer of books," wrote Fields many years later, "and in certain moods of mind it made very little difference what the volume before him happened to be."

In addition to literature he read a good deal of factual material, not only Froissart and Clarendon but such varied items as *The Newgate Calendar*, *The Gentleman's Magazine*, and Howell's *State Trials*. Many source studies have demonstrated his knowledge of American history. He read Macaulay with great interest, though he did not always agree with him. In biography he was torn between a fondness for the kind of realistic detail which the lover of human nature must relish and the shy or reserved man's dislike of the violation of privacy involved in supplying it. He was fond of travel books also, and he made considerable use of encyclopedias, anthologies, and compilations.[3]

Hawthorne's Biblical references and quotations are not numerous, but in view of his disinclination toward quotation in general, this is no evidence for lack of familiarity. Fields says that when his use of a word was questioned Hawthorne nearly always cited the Bible as his authority, that he was especially fond of the Book of Job, and that he repeated the words of the New Testament in a voice "tremulous with feeling." He once urged Fields to publish the Bible in a series of small volumes, thus making it easier to read.

His classical references are no more and no less than might have been expected of a man who had done well with Latin in college, but classical literature certainly meant much less to him than the Bible. In *A Wonder Book* and *Tanglewood Tales* he romanticized, Gothicized, and Christianized classical materials. (Only once, I think, in his description of Chiron in "The Golden Fleece," did he rationalize them.) We know that he realized exactly what he was doing, for he discussed the problems involved in some detail. What he objected to was not merely the "classic coldness" that repelled like "the touch of marble" but much more the fact that the tales themselves brimmed over with "everything that is most abhorrent to our Christianized moral sense." Since "no epoch of time can claim a copyright in these immortal fables," he made no apology for what he had done; instead he thought he had rewritten the stories "in excellent style, purified from all moral stains, re-created as good as new, or better, and fully equal, in their own way, to Mother Goose."

Chaucer was not greatly within the range of Hawthorne's knowledge, though he does refer to one young Englishman as a "Clerk of Oxenford." Julian says the family Chaucer was somewhat modernized. (We may be sure it was also bowdlerized.) With Shakespeare he did better. As a small child he went about spouting Richard III: "Stand back, my Lord, and let the coffin pass." He also read *The Tempest* with his cousin Lucy Sutton. *The Tempest* is quoted in *Grandfather's Chair*, and *As You Like It* is alluded to in *The Blithedale Romance*. He was unable to find any "foundation in nature" for *Love's Labour's Lost*, but he was very fond of *Cymbeline* and especially of Imogene, "the tenderest and womanliest woman that Shakespeare ever made immortal in the world." In "Earth's Holocaust" Shakespeare comes through the ordeal by fire very successfully.

Milton was quite as much a part of his thinking, for the Blithedale woods suggested "Comus" as well as *As You Like It*. He thought of "Lycidas" beside the Irish Sea and compared the United States after the loss of the South with heaven after Satan had drawn off the rebel angels. He dared to dislike Milton's heaven, however, not recognizing God in the portrait Milton drew of Him, and he did not care for Milton's prose, of which apparently he read little.

Spenser and Bunyan were greater influences upon him. *The Faerie Queene* was the first book Hawthorne bought with his own money; he named his first child from its pages; and he shared its enchantment with his children as soon as they were old enough to respond. Yet Julian says the first book from which the children ever heard him read aloud was *The Pilgrim's Progress*, and, if any one work must be chosen, Bunyan's masterpiece was probably Hawthorne's favorite book. It was the only work, too, upon which he ever composed a pastiche, and the high quality of "The Celestial Railroad" shows how closely attuned his mind was to Bunyan's. Matthiessen has noted "the extraordinary frequency with which memories of *Pilgrim's Progress* asserted themselves at moments when Hawthorne was creating his own most intense crises." [4]

The novelist who influenced him most was Sir Walter Scott. Scott's influence appeared first and most clearly in *Fanshawe*, where every feature of his technique was dutifully imitated: his use of epigraphs, his habit of throwing the scene back into the past, his weaving back and forth from one set of characters to another, and much besides. But even in *Fanshawe* Hawthorne had sense enough not to try to write about Scotland or about chivalry because Scott had written about them, as a lesser writer would have done; instead he applied Scott's methods and point of view to native New England materials.

George Edward Woodberry was right, I think, in seeing Scott's influence in Hawthorne's later fiction also—"in the figure-grouping, the high speeches, the oddities of character humorously treated, and especially in the use of set scenes individually elaborated to give the high lights and to advance the story." But Hawthorne's own later attitude toward Scott was as pernickety as E. M. Forster's. When he visited Abbotsford he was as difficult as only he knew how to be about sightseeing, and, though acknowledging how much Scott had done for his own youthful happiness, he felt that Sir Walter "could not have been really a wise man, nor an earnest one, nor one that grasped the truth of life." As early as "P's Correspondence," for that matter, he had treated Scott as a writer whose day was done. "The world, nowadays, requires a more earnest purpose, a deeper moral, and a closer and homelier truth than he was qualified to supply it with."

If Hawthorne sensed here that the future (insofar as we who shall someday be the past represent it) was to be more interested in the *Scarlet Letter*-type of novel than in the Scott-Cooper-Simms type, he was right, but it may be questioned whether the difference is a difference in earnestness and truth and homeliness rather than merely a difference in technique. Of course *The Scarlet Letter* itself is an historical novel only

in a very special sense. As an artist Hawthorne was not interested in history for history's sake. He criticized Simms severely
because he confined himself to "the lights and shades that lie
upon the surface of history." Such a writer, he said, cannot
cause "new moral shapes to spring up to the reader's mind." [5]
But it does not seem that Hawthorne ever really outgrew his
love for Scott. After his return to America, Ticknor and Fields
presented him with their new set of Scott; later they dedicated
their "Household Edition" of Lockhart's *Life* of Scott to him.
He at once set to work to read the Waverley Novels through
to his family, using them, it seems as a kind of refuge against
that Civil War which (since in attacking Scott no holds are
barred), Mark Twain was to accuse Scott of having caused.
The Lockhart dedication Hawthorne considered one of the
great honors of his life. "I do not deserve so high an honor;
but if you think me worthy, it is enough to make the compliment in the highest degree acceptable, no matter who may
dispute my title to it."

Stylistically, Scott was an eighteenth-century writer. And,
though there is a slighting reference to Pope in *The House of
the Seven Gables,* he was a pretty good eighteenth-century
man all his life. He was interested in Johnson and Swift from
his college days, though he qualified his admiration for Johnson almost as much as he did for Scott. He read and reread
Thomson's "Castle of Indolence," and he, somewhat surprisingly, called Sterne's sermons "the best ever written."

He read the great eighteenth-century novelists, too, apparently without the headshaking and handwringing popular in
his time, and of course he drew freely upon the paraphernalia
of the Gothic novelists for his supernaturalism. Godwin's
St. Leon probably exercised some influence upon *Septimius
Felton,* and one may hope that, when Hawthorne took the
name of Dr. Melmoth in *Fanshawe* from C. R. Maturin's

Melmoth the Wanderer, the greatest of the Gothic novels and the most neglected great novel in English literature, he recognized it for the distinguished work that it is.[6]

He knew the nineteenth-century novelists also, better, I think, than can now be documented. His sister Elizabeth claims that he read contemporary fiction very extensively during his Salem days with the idea of making "an artistic study" of it. He read *David Copperfield* aloud while it was still a new book, and there is an affectionate reference to Little Nell in "A Virtuoso's Collection," but it is my impression that Dickens meant less to him than to either Longfellow or Whittier. Maria Mitchell recorded his telling her that Thackeray was the greatest living novelist, but she "sometimes suspected that the volume of Thackeray was kept as a foil that he might not be talked to." He knew George Eliot and the Brontës also. He could not have read Charles Reade's *Griffith Gaunt* when it was serialized in the *Atlantic,* as Julian says, for he was dead, but Ada Shepard records his having read *It Is Never Too Late to Mend* to his family in 1857. One cannot but wonder whether it was Charlotte M. Yonge who contributed the name Redclyffe to *Dr. Grimshawe's Secret.*

It may seem surprising that a writer who so frankly recognized that his "native propensities were towards Fairy Land" should so greatly have admired the novels of Anthony Trollope. (Some have been equally surprised by Trollope's cordial admiration for Hawthorne.)[7]

They precisely suit my taste [thus Hawthorne to Fields, from England, concerning Trollope's novels]; solid and substantial, written on the strength of beef and through the inspiration of ale, and just as real as if some giant had hewn a great lump out of the earth and put it under a glass case, with all its inhabitants going about their daily business and not suspecting that they were made a show of.

This is quite in harmony with Hawthorne's "sensible" eighteenth-century side; he was an idealist and a dreamer, but he also knew that he was living in a material world. It is also in harmony with his tendency to disparage his own work, since he told Ticknor that if *The Marble Faun* had been written by somebody else he was not at all sure that he should like it. Like all writers Hawthorne did what he could. Like all writers who are also good critics, he appreciated the value of fine work in other modes. I do not believe that he ever *really* wanted to write like Trollope, and except when he was discouraged with himself he must have known that his own books had some excellent qualities which Trollope's lacked. But we must also remember that it is only the insensitive who find Trollope himself an insensitive writer, for all his beef and ale, and it is good to know that Hawthorne was not so insensitive as to make this mistake.

Towards poetry Hawthorne apparently determined to be as crotchety as possible. "I take vast satisfaction in your poetry," he writes Longfellow, "and very little in most other men's, except it be the grand old strains that have been sounding all through my life." Even when he sends William Allingham's poems to Ticknor for his consideration, he adds ungraciously, "I can't say that I have read them all, for I dislike poetry."

This does not seem to have been at all true in youth, and it is unlikely that it was ever really true. "I am full of scraps of poetry," he wrote at fifteen; "can't keep it out of my brain." As a youngster he even tried writing verses—"I could vomit up a dozen pages more if I were a mind to turn over." As a man he never attempted verse except, very occasionally, a piece of doggerel like the one about Bronson Alcott, the "sage at Apple-Slump."

On the other hand, Hawthorne declares that "a poet has a fragrance about him, such as no other human being is gifted withal." As "a seer, a revealer of internal truths, a prophet," he is "above contact with mere mortals." He was sure that only the poet's fame is worth having: Shakespeare did far more for Henry V than Henry V had ever done for him. Once he even called Sophia a poem:

Of what sort, then? Epic?—Mercy on me,—no! A sonnet?—no; for that is too labored and artificial. My Dove is a sort of sweet, simple, gay, pathetic ballad, which Nature is singing, sometimes with tears, sometimes with smiles, and sometimes with intermingled smiles and tears.

In his teens he waded through Sylvester's English version of *La Semaine* of du Bartas, and Sophia says that he often read in a 1791 edition of Charles Churchill's poems.[8] Such references may indicate a wider reading in the older English poets than Hawthorne is generally credited with. Rose thought her father did not care much for Tennyson, but Julian thought he did, and such references as we have support Julian. Browning he liked greatly as a man when they were together in Florence, but he seems to have been repelled by the difficulties of his poetry. When Mrs. Hawthorne returned to England from a stay in Portugal, he gave her Coventry Patmore's *The Angel in the House*, "saying that I should be refreshed and enchanted, and forget all my vexations in reading it." But when he thanked Ticknor for sending the book to him, he excepted from his appreciation "the lame-dromedary movement which poets nowadays seem so partial to."

The foreign references, too, are scattered enough to suggest considerable breadth. *Don Quixote*, *Gil Blas*, and *Le Diable Boiteux* were all discovered early. He speaks of Rabelais and of Molière. The Salem Athenaeum introduced him, partly at least in the original, to Voltaire, Rousseau, Pascal, Corneille, and Racine; and Elizabeth Peabody says that by 1837 he had read all the Balzac that had yet appeared. Both *Blithedale* and the *Faun* testify to his acquaintance with George Sand, and Cervantes, Rousseau, and Madame de Staël have all been cited as possible sources.[9]

American literature for Hawthorne was contemporary literature, much of it written by personal friends. He never wavered in his admiration for his old college mate Longfellow, in his view unquestionably the chief of American poets. He was particularly fond of *Evangeline*, and he admired the bold metrical experiment of *The Song of Hiawatha*, though he did not believe it would be popular. The only indication that he ever felt any weakness in Longfellow comes when he says that the poet seemed to him "no more conscious of any earthly or spiritual trouble than a sunflower is—of which lovely blossom he, I know not why, reminded me." He did not care greatly for Bryant, and his general opinion of Whittier's work was low. He was handicapped in his appreciation of Emerson's work by his lack of sympathy with the philosophy informing it. Poe could not have been wider of the mark than he was when he thought it necessary to advise Hawthorne to "hang (if possible) the editor of the *Dial*"; to Hawthorne *The Dial* was valuable chiefly as a soporific.[10]

His compliments to Irving and Cooper were graceful but conventional. In his early days he was fond of John Neal, and he gave Brockden Brown a place in "The Hall of Fantasy." He admired *Elsie Venner* and reread it shortly before his death. He gave his Berkshire neighbor Herman Melville his own little corner in *A Wonder Book*—"On the hither side of Pittsfield sits Herman Melville, shaping out the gigantic conception of the White Whale, while the gigantic shape of Graylock looms upon him from his study window." He was less sympathetic toward Poe, who was admitted to the original version of "The Hall of Fantasy" for his imagination but "threatened with ejectment, as belonging to the obnoxious class of critics."

In one of Hawthorne's notes to himself in the *Grimshawe* manuscript he was warned away from the theme of "remorse or secret guilt" on the ground that Poe had worn it out. This might be admiring or the reverse, but it does not show much understanding of Poe's aesthetic purpose. There is another passage in *Grimshawe*, however, in which we are informed that the "ghostly chord" has "been played upon, in these days, until it has become as nauseous as the familiar tune of a barrel organ." When Lord Houghton asked Hawthorne for half-a-dozen good American books, he suggested *Margaret* by Sylvester Judd, *Up Country Letters* by L. W. Mansfield, *Passion Flowers* by Julia Ward Howe, *Autobiography of an Actress* by Mrs. Mowatt, Thoreau's *Week* and *Walden*, and Lowell's *Fable for Critics* and *The Biglow Papers*, which last he admired in spite of his general distaste for Yankee dialect literature. At the end of his life he turned thumbs down on both Rebecca Harding Davis and Harriet Prescott Spofford, whose stories he thought both offensive and ill-written, but warmly welcomed Thomas Bailey Aldrich, whose poems he found "rich, sweet, and imaginative, in such a degree that I am sorry not to have fresher sympathies in order to taste all the delight that every reader ought to draw from them."

III

Of the other arts music was the one that meant least to Hawthorne. "Heaven be praised, I know nothing of music as a science; and the most elaborate harmonies, if they please me, please me as simply as a nurse's lullabies." The truth was that he had no ear "for an organ or a jewsharp nor any instrument between the two." He groups the drum and the fiddle together —"two ridiculous instruments"—and a well-intentioned English band which once played "Hail Columbia" in his honor as consul might just as well have played "God Save the Queen."

Yet, oddly enough, like many people who care nothing for music as such, he was extremely sensitive to the quality of the human voice. Take Arthur Dimmesdale at his Election sermon:

This vocal organ was in itself a rich endowment; insomuch that a listener, comprehending nothing of the language in which the preacher spoke, might still have been swayed to and fro by the mere tone and cadence. Like all other music, it breathed passion and pathos, and emotions high or tender, in a tongue native to the human heart, wherever educated.

The same sensitiveness appears in his analysis of the deficiencies of Hepzibah Pyncheon's voice, which, "naturally harsh, had, in the course of her sorrowful lifetime, contracted a kind of croak, which, when it once gets into the human throat, is as ineradicable as sin." And he goes on, with his rich artist's imagination, drawing upon every phase of the human animal's aesthetic endowment except a musical sensitivity:

The effect is as if the voice had been dyed black; or,—if we must use a more moderate simile,—this miserable croak, running through all the variations of the voice, is like a black silken thread, on which the crystal beads of speech are strung, and whence they take their hue. Such voices have put on mourning for dead hopes; and they ought to die and be buried along with them!

But when tenderness enters, even Hepzibah's poor voice can be transformed with

a plaintive and really exquisite melody thrilling through it, yet without subduing a certain something which an obtuse auditor might still have mistaken for asperity. It was as if some transcendent musician should draw a soul-thrilling sweetness out of a cracked instrument, which makes its physical imperfection heard in the midst of ethereal harmony,—so deep was the sensibility that found an organ in Hepzibah's voice!

Much more remarkable is the great description of the forest coven in "Young Goodman Brown," which has been orchestrated in its kind almost as elaborately as a tone poem by Richard Strauss.

Hawthorne did much better with the theater than with music. Indeed he did surprisingly well considering how limited his contacts with it were. He had too much imagination ever to share the Puritan dislike of the theater as such, and even in *Twice-Told Tales* the "I" of the "The Seven Vagabonds," relishing the puppet show, specifically disclaims "that foolish wisdom which reproves every occupation that is not useful in this world of vanities."

Apparently Hawthorne read a good deal of drama, not confining himself, as so many did, to Shakespeare and the Elizabethans. He took the name "Paul Pry" from a character in a play by John Poole thus titled (1825). He even attributes a fondness for reading modern plays to Septimius Felton, not too plausibly, one would think, in Revolutionary War Concord.

There are several references to theater-going in the letters Hawthorne wrote his mother and sister from Salem in 1820-21. In the spring of 1821 he was deeply moved by Edmund Kean's King Lear in Boston: "It was enough to have drawn tears from millstones. I could have cried myself, if I had been in a convenient place for such an exploit. I almost forget I did not live 'in Regis Learis seculum,' 'in the age of King Lear.'" The few dramatic reviews he wrote for the Salem *Advertiser* [11] show a surprisingly cultivated dramatic taste and sometimes, I am afraid, a tendency to be as cutting as certain metropolitan drama critics of today. In his early sketches he mentions Mrs. Siddons, Charles Matthews, John Philip Kemble, and Fanny Kemble, whom, of course, he knew in Lenox days. In England he saw Charles Kean in *Louis XI*, and he was disappointed upon arriving in Paris at the beginning of 1858 to learn that Rachel had just died.

I have no evidence that Hawthorne ever saw or heard any particular opera, but when, in 1858, he read in a newspaper the statement that *The Scarlet Letter* was being set to music, he remarked acutely, "I should think it might possibly succeed as an opera, though it would certainly fail as a play." [12] The "operatic" character of *The Scarlet Letter* has been remarked by a number of critics, and one does not need to be a very sophisticated reader to observe that the book develops itself in terms of a series of tableaux. Maurice Aaron Crane [13] has been impressed by the same thing in his study of *The Blithedale Romance*, which is full of "scenes" and full of specific allusions to the theater also—Hawthorne even says that he is turning the Brook Farm community into a theater—and whose heroine Zenobia is both conceived and presented in highly theatrical terms (what is the flower in her hair but a superb theatrical "property?") and given all the highlighting commonly reserved for the leading actress. Finally, Henry G. Fairbanks extends the tendency toward dramatic forms of presentation clear throughout Hawthorne's work:

> By extension the theatrical image is multiplied in Hawthorne's well-known penchant for dramatic groupings...; in his recurring tableaux, or set scenes; and in the generally heightened, rather than mimetic, quality of his dialogue. . . . His mastery of *chiaroscuro* owes much to an inclination to think in terms of stage-lighting.[14]

Hawthorne devoted a great deal of energy to thinking about the plastic arts. By 1858 he was even of the opinion that painting was capable of more magical effects than literature itself.

It is true that again and again in the Italian journals one is impressed by Mrs. Hawthorne's indefatigability in visiting museums and galleries compared with her husband's more limited appetite. "I was delighted not to have seen it," he writes. But though he may have rejected some areas wholesale—the Egyptian and the Assyrian, for example ("all full of monstrosities and horrible uglinesses")—his dislike of galleries indicates no indifference to art. He was simply too fastidious, too selective, and too highly individualistic to be able to take anything wholesale: "It seems to me that a picture, of all other things, should be by itself." Hawthorne's character was not, like that of Dickens or Theodore Roosevelt, notable for its gusto; as he himself recognized, his "receptive faculty" was "very limited," and when the cup was full it annoyed him to think that he might now perforce be rejecting the most valuable things of all.

It was in Europe that Hawthorne became really serious in his observation of art. How serious *The Marble Faun* shows, and it is not enough to view that novel as something merely overweighted with aesthetic appreciation copied out of Hawthorne's notebooks. Every stage in its development, every important idea expressed in it, is suggested by or symbolized by or embodied in a work of art, and the reactions and relationships of the characters to various works of art become a very important element in characterization. And whatever else Hawthorne may have intended by making Hilda a copyist rather than an original painter, one thing he certainly did intend to indicate—the girl's capacity for giving herself up to the great masters as the saints give themselves to God. Her painting is less self-expression than a form of devotion: she lends her brush, her hand, her eyes, her intuitions to the masters; through her sensitiveness the Spirit of Art extends itself in the world.

The great Exhibition of 1857 in Manchester marked a stage in Hawthorne's aesthetic education: "Positively I do begin to receive some pleasure from looking at pictures; but as yet it has nothing to do with any technical merit; nor do I think I shall ever get so far as that." Florence took him further: "In a year's time, with the advantage of access to this magnificent gallery, I think I might come to have some little knowledge of pictures." Then came Rome: "I am partly sensible that some unwritten laws of taste are making their way into my mind." Gamaliel Bradford once dedicated a novel with a Roman setting to his wife "in memory of the weary fascination of Rome." Hawthorne had felt both the weariness and the fascination. He was always conscious of the weight of the past but he felt it in Rome as he had never felt it elsewhere, and being as frank, if not so brash, as Mark Twain was later to be, he declared bluntly that much of the accumulation was rubbish. But he was also well aware that the Eternal City had tremendously stimulated his imagination.[15]

Yet Hawthorne's interest in art long antedated his European residence. "You cannot think how much delight those pictures you are painting are going to give me," he wrote Sophia during their courtship. "I never owned a picture in my life; yet pictures have been among the earthly possessions (and they are spiritual possessions too) which I most covet." This may be discounted as the expression of a young man's affection for a fiancée who is not only passionately interested in art but herself an artist, but it does not stand alone. From the beginning his stories were crammed with portraits. One, "The Prophetic Pictures," was based on an anecdote in Dunlap's *History of the Arts of Design*. Both "Drowne's Wooden Image" and "The Artist of the Beautiful" concern aesthetic problems. In *The Blithedale Romance* Hawthorne made Hollingsworth's failure to embrace art a part of his failure in life.

It has been repeatedly stated that Hawthorne was interested only in paintings which reproduce nature. As a matter of fact he knew even before he reached Italy that "nature cannot be exactly reproduced on canvas or in print; and the artist's only resource is to substitute something that may stand instead of and suggest the truth." He may forget this at times, as when he praises the Dutch painters for their minute fidelity, but in general he does insist upon selection and interpretation in painting and literature alike. The artist infuses his work with the light that never shone on sea or land except in his own heart and soul, and the reader's or the viewer's response depends helplessly on the harmony or lack of it between the artist's soul and his own.

The reverence and idealism which were such important elements in Hawthorne's basic constitution worked powerfully in the direction of winning his sympathy for the Italian masters, but his appreciation of them was sometimes inhibited by irrelevant considerations. When some "brazen trollop" of a painter's mistress was portrayed as the Madonna, for example, he found it difficult to believe that the religious sentiment intended was anything more than a veneer. Better the pipkins, kettles, and herrings of the Dutch masters than the pretence of religion.

Sometimes he would be deeply moved by one of the Old Masters, as once by

a large, dark, ugly picture of Christ bearing the cross and sinking beneath it, when somehow or other, a sense of his agony and the fearful wrong that mankind did to its Redeemer, and the scorn of his enemies and the sorrow of those who loved him, came knocking at my heart and partly got entrance there.

Generally, however, he could see nothing in the "ghastly decorations" of Giotto and Cimabue. Though these painters wrought with "care and conscientiousness," they did not aim at a "lifelike illusion," and they "might certainly be dismissed, henceforth and forever, without any detriment to the cause of good art." He was troubled too by the remarkable fact "that all the early faces of the Madonna are especially stupid, and all of the same type, a sort of face such as one might carve on a pumpkin, representing a heavy, sulky, phlegmatic woman, with a long and low arch of the nose." Furthermore, very early Italian paintings were generally available to Hawthorne's generation only in a state of decay, and while any other sort of ruin "acquires a beauty proper to its decay," he could not perceive that the ruin of a picture was good for anything. "Thank Heaven," he cries, "there is such a thing as whitewash; and I shall always be glad to hear of its application to old frescoes, even at the sacrifice of remnants of real excellence!"

Hawthorne greatly admired Murillo—"*my* painter," he once called him. "Murillo seems to me about the noblest and purest painter that ever lived, and his 'Good Shepherd' the loveliest picture I ever saw." Elsewhere Murillo's *St. John* is the only picture he would care to own, but he makes the same statement, contradictorily, at different times, about Raphael's *Transfiguration* and his *Madonna della Seggiola*. He loved Guido Reni's *Aurora*—"the picture is as fresh and brilliant as if he had painted it with the morning sunshine which it represents"—and his *Archangel Overcoming Lucifer*—"one of the human conceptions that are imbued most deeply with the celestial." Francia was praised for having approached his sacred subjects in the proper frame of mind. Hawthorne was greatly moved too by Sodoma's *Christ Bound*, for it seemed to him that the artist had almost "reconciled the impossibilities of combining an omnipresent divinity with a suffering and outraged humanity."

He was cold to Michelangelo's paintings, though acknowledging their greatness, and he never did quite make up his mind about the cartoons and preliminary sketches of Raphael, Leonardo, and Michelangelo. Sometimes he thought such things could be of interest only to other artists, and sometimes he found a greater charm in them than in the finished picture; "that is to say, they bring me much closer to the hands that drew them and the minds that imagined them. It is like looking into their brains, and seeing the first conception before it took place outwardly." He showed a tendency to disparage Titian, generally on moral grounds: only the *Bella Donna* "makes an impression on me corresponding with his fame." He did not think Daniele de Volterra's *The Descent from the Cross* worth looking at, though he had been told that it was the third greatest picture in the world, and he found Carlo Dolce's "portrait of the Eternal Father" ridiculous.

It is the All-powerless, a fair-haired, soft, consumptive deity, with a mouth that has fallen open through very weakness. He holds one hand on his stomach, as if the wickedness and wretchedness of mankind had made him qualmish; and he is looking down out of heaven with an expression of pitiable appeal, as if asking somewhere for assistance in the heavy task of running the universe.

Van Dyck's picture of Charles I—"a figure and face of melancholy dignity as never by any other hand was put on canvas"—so impressed Hawthorne that he felt as though he had seen the king in person. And nowhere did he differentiate more clearly between his interest in the subject and in the picture, between what the painter took from nature and what he created:

Yet, on considering this face of Charles . . . and translating it from the ideal into literalism, I doubt whether the unfortunate king was really a handsome or impressive-looking man: a high, thin-ridged nose, a meagre, hatchet face, and reddish hair and beard, —these are the literal facts. It is the painter's art that has thrown such pensive and shadowy grace around him.

The realistic Dutch and Flemish painters in general Hawthorne admired for the same reason that he enjoyed Trollope's novels: they were "men of flesh and blood and warm fists and human hearts." In comparison the great Italians seemed "men of polished steel; not human, nor addressing themselves so much to human sympathies as to a formed, intellectual taste."

Hawthorne enjoyed Hogarth but he could not endure Turner—"I care no more for his light-colored pictures than for so much lacquered ware or painted gingerbread"—and he thought English painters in general quite unable to produce anything "high, heroic, and ideal." Lawrence's grace was a kind of trick, and therefore disgusting, and Reynolds was not quite genuine either. Haydon he respected not for his pictures, "they being detestable to see," but for his high and, for him, unattainable ends. In Haydon's *Resurrection of Lazarus* he found the face of the central figure "very awful, and not to be forgotten," but the rest of the picture was "vulgar and disagreeable." For the Pre-Raphaelites he had a certain respect, and toward their future achievement he looked with a kind of hope, but they also gave him the impression of trying to make their pictures as disagreeable as possible "out of mere malice."

As for American painters, Hawthorne had been deeply interested in the portraits at the Essex Historical Society in Salem as far back as 1837, but he thought he would rather look at a basilisk than the pictures in the Boston Athenaeum! There is an admiring reference to Washington Allston in "The Artist of the Beautiful," but he greatly disliked Nathaniel West, who had "a gift of frigidity, a knack of grinding ice into his paint, a power of stupefying the spectator's perceptions and quelling his sympathy, beyond any other limner that ever handled a brush." Among his contemporaries he greatly admired C. G. Thompson.

In a very special sense, Hawthorne's favorite picture was Guido Reni's *Beatrice Cenci*, which fascinated him as it fascinates Hilda in *The Marble Faun*. In a way he fell in love with the subject; in a way she repelled him. Above all she tormented him because he could not fathom her secret.

The hideous old story of incest and parricide in which the

real Beatrice Cenci was presumed to have played her part has its hold on him here, and he says frankly that he cannot tell what effect the picture would have on somebody who came to it without prepossessions.

Yesterday afternoon we went to the Barberini picture-gallery to take a farewell look at the Beatrice Cenci, which I have twice visited before since our return from Florence. I attempted a description of it at my first visit, more than a year ago, but the picture is quite indescribable and unaccountable in its effect, for if you attempt to analyze it you can never succeed in getting at the secret of its fascination. Its peculiar expression eludes a straightforward glance, and can only be caught by side glimpses, or when the eye falls upon it casually as it were, and without thinking to discover anything, as if the picture had a life and consciousness of its own, and were resolved not to betray its secret of grief or guilt, though it wears the full expression of it when it imagines itself unseen. I think no other such magical effect can ever have been wrought by pencil. I looked close into its eyes, with a determination to see all that there was in them, and could see nothing that might not have been in any young girl's eyes; and yet, a moment afterwards, there was the expression—seen aside, and vanishing in a moment —of a being unhumanized by some terrible fate, and gazing at me out of a remote and inaccessible region, where she was frightened to be alone, but where no sympathy could reach her. The mouth is beyond measure touching; the lips apart, looking as innocent as a baby's after it has been crying. The picture never can be copied. Guido himself could not have done it over again. The copyists get all sorts of expression, gay as well as grievous; some copies have a coquettish air, a half-backward glance, thrown alluringly at the spectator, but nobody ever did catch, or ever will, the vanishing charm of that sorrow. I hated to leave the picture, and yet was glad when I had taken my last glimpse, because it so perplexed and troubled me not to be able to get hold of its secret.

Hawthorne's interest in *Beatrice Cenci* was basically an interest in the mysteries of human character, but if the painter's achievement had been less his interest would not have been stimulated as it was. He did not know enough about technique to be able to explain how the effect was secured (if anybody can), but unless we are prepared to read art and technique as synonymous terms, or commit ourselves to the view that painters paint for the critics and for other painters, it will be difficult to deny that Hawthorne was one of those for whom Guido Reni's portrait of Beatrice Cenci was painted and in relation to whom it fulfilled its purpose.

It has been said that sculpture meant more to Hawthorne than painting. There is no real evidence to substantiate this view, though there were times when he was inclined to think of sculpture as more "genuine" than painting because it was more inevitable and closer to nature. Certainly sculpture was in Hawthorne's eyes a very noble art, making high demands upon both the beholder and the creator, and he showed his high regard for it in his feeling that the sculptor must either succeed gloriously or egregiously fail: there was no stopping place between "a celestial thing" and "an old lump of stone, dusty and time-soiled." Since it involved also a relative permanence he felt that marble should never be dedicated to subjects unworthy of being permanently preserved. No picture, not even *Beatrice Cenci*, gave Hawthorne as much for his art as the Faun of Praxiteles, and the *Venus de Medici* probably meant as much to him as the *Beatrice Cenci*, though in a less psychological way.[16]

The *Apollo Belvidere*, the *Laocoön*, the *Marcus Aurelius* on the Capitoline Hill, Canova's *Perseus*, and John of Bologna's *Mercury* are among the statues praised by Hawthorne, and Frank Stearns cites his appreciation of the statues of Castor and Pollux on the Quirinal as evidence that he did not confine his appreciation to conventional things and that in this instance his taste was in advance of its time. In some cases, however, his impressions and evaluations varied greatly with his moods.

"I saw the Apollo Belvidere as something ethereal and godlike; only for a flitting moment, however, and as if he had alighted from heaven, or shone suddenly out of the sunlight, and then had withdrawn himself again." This is one of several indications of Hawthorne's realization that art lives in the eye of the beholder.

Michelangelo apparently impressed him more as sculptor than as painter, since he calls his *Lorenzo de Medici* "the greatest miracle ever wrought in marble." He knew many contemporary American sculptors in Rome, and he seems to have admired many of them, though he could see nothing in Thomas Crawford (who had died in 1857). He "boomed" W. W. Story's *Cleopatra* by describing it at length in *The Marble Faun*.

Hawthorne's love for Gothic architecture was passionate.

A Gothic cathedral is surely the most wonderful work which mortal man has yet achieved, so vast, so intricate, and so profoundly simple, with such strange, delightful recesses in its grand figure, so difficult to comprehend within one idea, and yet all so consonant that it ultimately draws the beholder and his universe into its harmony. It is the only thing in the world that is vast enough and rich enough.

When he first saw Lichfield Cathedral it seemed "the object best worth gazing at in the whole world," while York was "the most wonderful work that ever came from the hands of man." And he thanks God that he has seen it and that God inspired the builder to construct it.

In *The Marble Faun* we may be sure that Kenyon is speaking for Hawthorne when he expresses his pity for all Christians who must pass through life

"without once seeing an antique painted window, with the bright Italian sunshine glowing through it! There is no other such true symbol of the glories of the better world, where a celestial radiance will be inherent in all things and persons, and render each continually transparent to the sight of all."

Hawthorne's, too, is Kenyon's questioning of Milton's "dim, religious light":

"I always admired this richly descriptive phrase; but, though he was once in Italy, I question whether Milton ever saw any but the dingy pictures in the dusty windows of English cathedrals, imperfectly shown by the gray English daylight. He would else have illuminated that word 'dim' with some epithet that should not chase away the dimness, yet should make it glow like a million of rubies, sapphires, emeralds, and topazes."

There was never any question in Hawthorne's mind that he preferred Gothic architecture to classical, which was "nothing but an outline."

I admire this in Gothic architecture,—that you cannot master it all at once and that it is not a naked outline, but as deep and rich as human nature itself, always revealing new ideas. It is as if the builder had built himself and his age up into it, and as if the edifice had life. Grecian edifices are very uninteresting to me, being so cold and crystalline.

That he did not, however, automatically reject all non-Gothic ecclesiastical architecture may be seen by his response to St. Paul's:

What a total and admirable contrast between this and a Gothic church! the latter so dim and mysterious, with its various aisles, its intricacy of pointed arches, its dark walls and columns and pavement, and its painted glass windows, bedimming even what daylight might otherwise get into its eternal evening. But this cathedral was full of light, and light was proper to it. There were no painted windows, no dim recesses, but a wide and airy space beneath the dome; and even through the long perspective of the nave there was no obscurity, but one lofty and beautifully rounded arch succeeding to another, as far as the eye could reach. The walls were white, the pavements constructed of squares of gray and white marble. It is a most grand and stately edifice, and its characteristic seems to be to continue forever fresh and new; whereas such a church as Westminster Abbey must have been as venerable as it is now from the first day when it grew to be an edifice at all. How wonderful man is in his works! How glad I am that there can be two such admirable churches in their opposite style, as St. Paul's and Westminster Abbey!

Hawthorne did not foresee the American Gothic revival in ecclesiastical architecture. He had the feeling that architecture should be an expression of the spirit of the country, and he was always suspicious of following ancient fashions; Elizabethan-style houses in America struck him as an "affectation." In his *American Magazine* days at least he felt that the "simplicity of our faith, divested as it is of those elaborate inventions, which being of earthly origin, require an earthly grandeur in everything connected with them," required also "a simpler style of architecture" than prevailed elsewhere.

Hawthorne does not anywhere specifically state that he realized that the Gothic cathedral was as much the natural or inevitable architectural expression of the Christian faith and attitude toward life as the Greek temple was natural and inevitable for those who possessed the spiritual nature of the Greeks. But William M. White has observed [17] that "in siding with the Gothic the romancer pledges allegiance to those elements which are grandiose, mysterious, and suggestive in life. . . . He elects the imagination over the reason, intuition over intellective knowledge." Hawthorne also knew that the irregularity of the Gothic brought it closer to human experience than the smoothed and stylized classical. If Professor White is right, as I think he is, then Hawthorne preferred the Gothic both for its aspiration and for its realism, and this would be quite in harmony with his feeling that the Christian religion alone recognizes the truth about human nature and at the same time provides man with a means of rising above it.

But what, now, of the most important thing of all—Hawthorne's practice of his own art?

George Edward Woodberry, who divides with W. C. Brownell the functions of devil's advocate among Hawthorne's older critics, once remarked that Hawthorne probably drifted into authorship through a disinclination to do anything else. Woodberry was too good a critic not to know that writing of Hawthorne's quality cannot be produced to order but must proceed from the deepest levels of a writer's being. It is true, however, that there is an 1821 letter from Hawthorne to his mother in which he seems to be reaching his profession by a process of elaborate exclusion ("What do you think of my becoming an author, and relying for my support upon my pen?"), and it must be admitted that it is difficult to think of anything else he might have done which would have satisfied him as writing did. But all this would seem to indicate rather that Hawthorne *was* made for his art than that he was not.

Since both of Hawthorne's sisters were interested in writing, he had, in a way, a literary atmosphere around him. He wrote in childhood; he wrote much more seriously at college.[18] Did he then desire fame? He denies it. "The bubble reputation is as much a bubble in literature as in war," he wrote Bridge in 1851, "and I should not be one whit the happier if mine were world-wide and time-long than I was when nobody but yourself had faith in me." "In this dismal chamber fame was won," he wrote satirically of his old room in Salem in 1835, and when he revisited it eight years later he turned out a burlesque of what pious literary pilgrims might some day come to say there:

"There," they will exclaim, "is the very bed in which he slumbered, and where he was visited by those ethereal visions which

he afterwards fixed forever in glowing words! There is the wash-
stand at which this exalted personage cleansed himself from the
stains of earth, and rendered his outward man a fitting exponent
of the pure soul within."

Even as late as *Marble Faun* days he tells Fields "that I am
not really a popular writer, and that what popularity I have
gained is chiefly accidental, and owing to other causes than
my own kind or degree of merit." But it should be noted that
he quickly adds, "Possibly I may (or may not) deserve something better than popularity."

But he responded to discriminating praise. "I really do not
think that I like to be praised *viva voce;* at least, I am glad
when it is said and done with, though I will not say that my
heart does not expand a little towards the man who rightly
appreciates my books." To be sure he complains that the S. C.
Halls "besmeared me with such sweetness of laudation, that I
feel all over bestuck, as after handling sweetmeats or molasses-
candy." But he felt kindly toward the Halls nevertheless. He
was pleased when a Lyceum lecturer at Salem went out of his
way to praise him. He was pleased when he learned that a
commencement oration at Wesleyan had been devoted to his
work. He was pleased with the recognition accorded him in
London, and when he was introduced to Lincoln he seems to
have been hurt that the President had obviously never heard
of him.[19]

He seems always to have replied courteously to letters of
appreciation from strangers, requests for autographs, etc. He
sent Elizabeth Peabody a copy of *Twice-Told Tales* in appreciation of her interest even before they had met. In 1852 a man
in Keokuk, Iowa, wrote asking three things, "first, to send him
a copy of the Life of Pierce; secondly, to accompany the same
with all my other works;—and thirdly, to place him on the list
of regular correspondents!" Hawthorne was well aware of the

enormity of this procedure but, thinking it "a pity" that his correspondent "should not obtain some small percentage of all these modest requests," he directed Fields to send him the *Life of Pierce*. In an 1863 letter to Robert I. Powy he goes to an extreme in minimizing the difference between the writer's contribution to the success of a work of art and the reader's:

> But you attribute to me a superiority which I do not dream of asserting. A reader, who can fully understand and appreciate a work, possesses all the faculties of the writer who produces it —except a knack of expression, by which the latter is enabled to give definite shape to an idea or sentiment which he and his appreciative reader possess in common. Thus the advantage on the author's part is but a slight one, and the more truth and wisdom he writes, the smaller is his individual share of it.

In his estimate of what he had actually accomplished as a writer Hawthorne was never arrogant. He seems to have been painfully impressed by the hardships of the writer's career: he advised Julian against it, and when George William Curtis "arrived," he told him he was glad "for the sake of the public but not particularly for your own." Sometimes he professed not to be able to understand his own work.

Obviously he must have believed in his books while he was writing them; otherwise he would have given up. At the end he struggled with the (in his state of health) insuperable difficulties of *Septimius Felton* and *Dr. Grimshawe's Secret* long past the point of diminishing returns. He has often been blamed for preferring *The House of the Seven Gables* to *The Scarlet Letter*, and especially for his stubborn wilfulness in maintaining that the quite unnecessary introductory sketch of "The Custom House" (so hopelessly out of harmony with the tone of the novel itself) was what had made *The Scarlet Letter* a success. But, as Miss Faust has shown,[20] these ideas seem much more absurd to us than they did to contemporary critics, who were always inclined to place *The House of the Seven Gables* higher than *The Scarlet Letter* and *The Marble Faun* ahead of both. *The Scarlet Letter* must have seemed even darker to Hawthorne than it does to us, for it was his first long fiction, associated with all the doubts and problems which beset a first attempt, and associated besides with both the death of his mother and the loss of his own position in the custom house. Nor will it do to pretend that he did not understand what he had created, for he was overcome by his own emotion when he read the manuscript to his wife.

He had his difficulties with the *Seven Gables* too:

> Sometimes, when tired of it, it strikes me that the whole is an absurdity, from beginning to end; but the fact is, in writing a romance, a man is always, or always ought to be, careening on the utmost verge of a precipitous absurdity, and the skill lies in coming as close as possible, without actually tumbling over.

On *The Marble Faun*, as might from its nature have been expected, he vacillated more. He "admired it exceedingly at intervals," but he was also "liable to cold fits" during which he thought it "the most infernal nonsense."

Fields thought Hawthorne an easy author to deal with, but he knew what an author's rights were and maintained them. "Perhaps you will not like it," he wrote one editor; "if so, make no ceremony about rejecting it. I am as tractable an author as you ever knew, so far as putting my articles into the fire goes; though I cannot abide alterations or omissions." When Fields insisted upon taking the sketch of Lincoln out of "Chiefly About War Matters" in the *Atlantic*, he yielded but made it perfectly clear that he thought Fields wrong and that should he reprint the article in a book he would restore the excised material. He sent *The Blithedale Romance* to E. P. Whipple for criticism but he did not promise to change anything in response to his suggestions: "the metal hardens very

soon after I pour it out of my melting pot into the mould."
When he was accused of having taken an idea for "Dr. Heidigger's Experiment" from a novel by Dumas, he added a note to
the next printing in which he pointed out that, since his story
was older than the novel, the alleged plagiarism could not
possibly have been on his part.[21]

Despite Hawthorne's unmistakable sincerity in everything
connected with literature he sometimes gives the impression
of half-heartedness. On June 1, 1846, Longfellow met him in
George Hillard's office. "He walked with me to the bridge and
half across," the Cambridge poet confided to his journal. "He
seemed weary of most men and things; and having obtained an
office in the Salem Custom House, I fear he will grow idle
in literature." He never could write unless the conditions were
favorable. Even as a boy he told his mother that he could not
be a writer and a bookkeeper at the same time. Shortly after
accepting the Salem post he wrote E. A. Duyckinck that "my
office (the duties of it being chiefly performable by deputy)
will allow me as much time for literature as can be profitably
applied." But he did not write during this period; instead he
says that literary matters passed entirely out of his mind. He
never wrote when he had anything else to do. He could not
write at Brook Farm. He could not write in Italy. He did not
even write while The Wayside was being enlarged and altered.
And wherever he was he never felt able to do anything until
after the first frost. Even the *prospect* of other employment
seems to have been fatal to literature, and at the Old Manse
we find him saying, "I might have written more, if it had
seemed worth while; but I was content to earn only so much
gold as might suffice for our immediate wants, having prospect
of official station and emolument which would do away with
the necessity of writing for bread."

This seems almost as skittish a muse as that of the German

poet who could only write with the odor of decayed bananas
in the room, but, though Hawthorne may have been somewhat
lethargic, I doubt that there was any affectation in his attitude.
Lacking Trollope's hold on common things, he also lacked
Trollope's superb control of his resources. As early as 1844
he knew that he could not spend more than one-third of his
time in creative work:

> It requires a continual freshness of mind, else a deterioration in
> the article will quickly be perceptible. If I am to support myself
> by literature, it must be by what is called drudgery, but which
> is incomparably less irksome as a business, than imaginative writing
> —by translation, concocting of school-books, newspaper scribbling,
> etc.

His muse was a jealous mistress who must be served for
disinterested motives or not at all. "Yet, after all, I must keep
these considerations out of my mind, because an external purpose always disturbs, instead of assisting me." Under other
conditions he might have turned for bread to utilitarian writing rather than to the completely non-literary kind of work
he did do; we shall never know whether his creative work
would have profited by this or suffered from it. At one time
there was under consideration a plan to do some fairy stories
for children in collaboration with Longfellow. In 1842 he was
willing to consider an editorial position.[22]

Hawthorne swings back and forth between the practical life
and the aesthetic life as if he were not so much balancing one
against the other as using each as a refuge from the other.
In England in 1854 he went so far as to speak of "my literary
avocations"; the very next year the pen is "my legitimate instrument." But in spite of such statements as "the more I use a
pen, the worse I hate it," and in spite of his profession that
he had only commercial motives for writing during his last
years, there is not much question that, like Cynara's lover,

he was always faithful after his fashion. He had enough of the practical Yankee in him to be aware of the danger of being drawn away, through art, from the realities of life, but when he was at his best he knew too that the life of the artist was the only life that was real for him. "I have been writing about another man's consular experiences," he remarks in *Our Old Home*, "with which, through some mysterious medium of transmitted ideas, I find myself intimately acquainted, but in which I cannot possibly have had a personal interest." [23]

Like other writers, Hawthorne got his ideas everywhere —from experience, from observation, from reading. But though he was never the D. H. Lawrence, cathartic, "art-for-my-sake" kind of writer, neither was he much given to the use of materials quite unconnected with his own personal, vital interests. He contemplated several romances founded on old English state trials and another based on the Rich Young Ruler in the New Testament, but he wrote none of these. On the other hand, he could write his own child into *The Scarlet Letter* (even if he had to bastardize her in the process), and there seems to be a good deal of material out of the Hawthorne household in "The Dolliver Romance." In *The Blithedale Romance* he daringly reminds the reader of Margaret Fuller and at the same time guards against her identification with Zenobia.

George Eliot found Zenobia's suicide and its aftermath "an outrage upon the decorum of art, as well as a violation of its purpose." [24] I wonder what she would have said if she had read the corresponding passage in *The American Notebooks* in which Hawthorne describes how he helped recover the body of Martha Hunt from the Concord River.[25] A careful study of the differences and resemblances between the two constitutes one of the best examples I know of how the raw material of experience may be transmuted into art.

Hawthorne used a thousand passages from his notebooks in this way, but they all suffered a sea change in the process, much more than George Eliot's Italian learning did before she dumped it into *Romola*. For the world of Hawthorne's stories is a created realm in which he and he alone has served as demi-urge. "I thought of Mr. Pickwick," said Dickens when giving an account of the origin of *The Pickwick Papers*. In that sense Hawthorne never "thought" of anybody. He begins with an idea or an impression; the characters enter later as an embodiment of it. He arranges them in groups and high-lights them like a painter (he tends to favor groups of four); they relate themselves in terms of symmetry to the "central event" of the novel and to its well-spaced "scenes."

It is no wonder, then, that Hawthorne has, time and again, been compared to Henry James (he was the only important American influence upon James's art) and more recently to Faulkner. Canby sees in a notebook sketch what might have been the germ of Eugene O'Neill's *Dynamo;* Cameron com-pares "The Ambitious Guest" with *The Bridge of San Luis Rey;* Conrad, Lawrence, Kafka, Hemingway, and Robert Penn Warren have also been named.[26] And it is significant that, different as they are, none of these are realistic or naturalistic writers. All are more interested in the "soul" or in the essence of human character than they are in showing the very age and body of the time his form and pressure. A number of them might say with Hawthorne himself, "Our story is an internal one." Several are impressionistic or expressionistic in their technique.[27]

As everybody knows, Hawthorne thought of his own books as "romances," not novels. He turned away from the life all around him in the custom house to the old Boston of *The Scarlet Letter*. In *The House of the Seven Gables* he proposed to adhere to "the truth of the human heart" but to present it "under circumstances, to a great extent, of the writer's own choosing or creation." His concern with "the socialist community" of *The Blithedale Romance*, though he had lived in it, was "merely to establish a theatre, a little removed from the highway of ordinary travel, where the creatures of his brain may play their phantasmagorical antics, without exposing them to too close a comparison with the actual events of real lives." And finally, in *The Marble Faun*, Italy afforded "a sort of poetic precinct, where actualities would not be so terribly insisted upon as they are, and must needs be, in America," a land "where there is no shadow, no antiquity, no mystery, no picturesque and gloomy wrong, nor anything but a commonplace prosperity, in broad and simple daylight."

It may be that Hawthorne turned to romance at the outset, as Mark Van Doren suggests, because he had not had sufficient experience to write anything else. But since he was not interested in the surface of life but in life's essence and meaning, what else could he do? Like Virginia Woolf, he was less concerned with Mrs. Brown than with "Mrs. Brownness." He had always been more fascinated by what is reflected in a mirror than by what the mirror reflects. How could it be otherwise, since a mirror is "a kind of window or doorway into the spiritual world"? He knew, too, that the meaning of experience cannot be intelligently apprehended until it has been seen in perspective and that perspective requires distance and a degree of disinterestedness. How, then, could he have avoided the past?

Hawthorne formulated no such apologetic for romanticism as did Robert Louis Stevenson or James Branch Cabell or Walter de la Mare. But he knew, quite as well as de la Mare knew it, that there is a difference between "matter-of-fact" and "matter-of-truth," and he knew too (though he would not have used the same vocabulary), that realism "in the accepted sense" is only "a kind of scientific reporting" and that "an imaginative experience is not only as real but far realer than an unimaginative one."

All artists know this whether they know that they know it or not. But those who know that they know it are always likely to be bolder and more skillful in their technique than those who do not. When I speak of Hawthorne's passion to penetrate to essentials, I do not mean that he was a moralist (though, to be sure, he sometimes was). Realistic aims and techniques do not inhibit moralizing, and Hawthorne was considerably less didactic than he is generally considered to have been. It was not the moralist who got well into "Rappaccini's Daughter" without making up his mind about the girl's character or knowing how the story would end, and it was not the moralist who advised Mrs. Richard Henry Stoddard to let the morals of her stories take care of themselves. Hawthorne did not impress contemporary critics as a moralist. They complained that, while he had "a rich and fine perception of the beautiful," he was "sadly deficient in moral depth and earnestness," "morbid as well as weak" in "moral faculty." He was criticized for not meting out rewards and punishments to his characters and called "a Mephistopheles, doubtful whether to weep or laugh." Indeed "the moral of some of his books" was "not only not moral, but positively immoral."

Of course this is stupid, undiscerning criticism, but no more so than that written by those of our contemporaries who cannot distinguish between patient probing for the meaning of experience and teaching "lessons." The first kind of writer submits himself to his material—and to life; the other, in a sense, stands aside from both. He has all the answers ready beforehand, and he pastes them on like labels. If the labels do not suit the bottles he may change the contents slightly, or, more likely, he will send them out mislabeled. Hawthorne does not flee the

real for the ideal; he seeks the ideal in the real. To disengage
it he sloughs off accident and contradiction. He is a good
Aristotelian in this. Even when he deals with the local materials he knew best, he universalizes. He was no more concerned
to document New England history in the *Twice-Told Tales*
than in *The Scarlet Letter*, and when he uses the trappings of
Gothic romance, these too are but a means toward an end.
In one place he himself says that though his "ground-plots"
rarely lie "within the widest scope of probability," they still
respect "homely and natural" truth. If he was committed to
anything in the way of method, he was committed to the use
of symbols, but even this was only a means of bringing meaning into focus. In themselves his symbols were of no more use
to him than the "slice of life" would have been had it been
his misfortune to live long enough to encounter that method.
If he had ever doubted any of this, he learned its truth at the
end, when he failed to complete *Septimius Felton* and *Dr.
Grimshawe's Secret*, because, though he could still conjure up
symbols to his heart's content, he was no longer able to find
anything for them to symbolize.[28]

CHAPTER THREE

NATURE AND HUMANITY

I

A writer writes about people, and in addition to writing about them he has to live with them. How did Hawthorne fare in this aspect?

In the nineteenth century the nature cult was so influential that many persons turned to nature for what ordinarily we expect from our fellow men, so that even in Hawthorne's own Concord, Emerson somewhat unfairly told Thoreau that if God had intended him to live in a swamp He would have made him a frog. Some even made nature a surrogate for religion. By way of preliminary to the consideration of Hawthorne's relationship with humanity, it might, then, be well to attempt first to define his attitude toward nature.

Hawthorne had abundant opportunity to learn to love nature during that portion of his boyhood which he spent in the Maine woods. He never threw off this conditioning, and we are told that when he lived at the Old Manse he never stayed indoors except in bad weather. He skated; he boated; he bathed. "I get up at sunrise to skate!!!!!!!!!!!!" he wrote Long-fellow. The "thrillingly cold" water of Walden Pond, "like the thrill of a happy death," was a bathing place fit for angels. "It would be a fit bathing-place for my little wife." Once he and Thoreau floated down the Concord River on an ice-cake, towing their boat behind them.

Nobody who knows the great forest chapters in *The Scarlet*

Letter will need to be told that Hawthorne did not always escape the pathetic fallacy. But he was much less seduced by it than many of his contemporaries; perhaps the terrible winter of his boyhood when two of his Maine neighbors froze to death in a blizzard took care of such things for him.

Nothing comes amiss to nature—all is fish that comes to her net. If there be a living form of perfect beauty instinct with soul, —why, it is all very well, and suits Nature well enough. But she would just as lief have that same beautiful soul-illumined body, to make worm's meat of, and to manure the earth with.[1]

Yet he felt the importance of keeping in tune with nature; perversion horrified him, whether it took the form of an Egyptian mummifying process or of Dr. Rappaccini's unholy experiments with plants. He might even have been horrified by Luther Burbank. In the early days at least he preferred a vessel "that voyaged in the good old way, by favor of the wind, instead of one that tears her passage through the deep in spite of wind and tide, snorting and groaning, as if tormented by the fire that rages in her entrails." And his preference for the fireplace over the stove as expressed in "Fire Worship" anticipates Charles Dudley Warner's whimsy in *Backlog Studies*.

In general, Hawthorne craved the association of human life with nature: he liked apple trees for their suggestion of domesticity and friendliness toward man, as, later, he loved the quiet, medium-sized, domesticated natural beauty of the English countryside. He even preferred Concord's "broad and peaceful meadows," with the sluggish Concord River winding its way among them, to the more spectacular scenery of the Berkshires, which tended to "stamp and stereotype" itself into his brain and thus became "wearisome with the same strong impression, repeated day by day." The small wild ridge above The Wayside, where he paced among the larches as long as he was capable of walking anywhere, was a solace and comfort to the end.

Yet he loved the sea, loved to live beside it, as he did in Salem, and loved his small experience in sailing upon it. He even wanted to go through a storm at sea "if I were sure of getting safe to dry land at last"!

"No trees, I think, are perfectly agreeable as companions unless they have glossy leaves, dark bark, and a firm and hard texture of trunk and branches." He did not care for willows. Flowers seem to have meant surprisingly little to him. In *Septimius Felton* he dismisses dahlias as lacking "deep characteristics." Lathrop says that the lily-of-the-valley was his favorite. Of his wife he once wrote, "She has, in perfection, this love and taste for flowers, without which a woman is a monster and which it would be well for men to possess, if they can."

After coming to the Old Manse, Hawthorne found "the natural taste of man for the original Adam's occupation" developing in him rapidly. Gathering his first string beans gave him "a very pleasant moment." He felt "as if something were being created under my own inspection, and partly my own aid."

Summer squashes are a very pleasant vegetable to be acquainted with:—they grow in the forms of urns and vases, some shallow, others of considerable depth, and with a beautifully scalloped edge. Almost any squash in our garden might be copied by a sculptor, and would look beautifully in marble, or in china ware, and if I could afford it, I would have exact imitations of the real vegetable as portions of my dining service. . . . Except a pumpkin, there is no vegetable production that imparts such an idea of warmth and comfort to the beholder.

He had happy relations with birds and animals. His observations of poultry in *The House of the Seven Gables* are worthy of Chaucer, and he once told Bridge that he felt like a cannibal when he ate his own chickens. Chaucerian, too, are his descriptions of bird-song in "Buds and Bird Voices"—"their outburst of melody . . . like a brook let loose from wintry chains," their "hymn of praise to the Creator"—and his nice discriminations between them. But his crow suggests Mark Twain rather than Chaucer. "A crow . . . has no real pretensions to religion, in spite of their gravity of mien and black attire; they are certainly thieves and probably infidels." He fed and helped birds when they needed it, and he admired them when, like the sea gulls, they sailed above his head, free of all human dependence.

At the Old Manse Hawthorne and Sophia did not miss people, but they did feel that they needed animals, at least a kitten. "Animals (except, perhaps, a pig) seem never out of place, even in the most paridisiacal spheres." I do not know why the poor pig should be excluded, nor why the monkey should typify evil in *The House of the Seven Gables*, but Hawthorne seems to have felt that monkeys were a kind of parody or diabolical caricature of humanity. His attitude toward pigs was evidently not one of settled hostility; in one passage in *The American Notebooks* they are a revolting type of sensuality, but in another he professes "great sympathy and interest for the whole race" and much curiosity about their "character." Cows had "character" for him too, for he thought Margaret Fuller's beast had "a very intelligent face" and "a reflective cast" of mind. He seems to have taken a dim view of the eel, the frog, and the turtle, but he gives Peter Goldthwaite a Burns-like tenderness for the rats and mice whom his operations disturb, and Hawthorne himself, though without compunctions about killing a fly in the house, felt mean about doing it in his own domain, the open air.

Hawthorne made a detailed record of his relations with Julian's "Bunny." I am not sure how much it shows about

Bunny but it shows a good deal about Hawthorne. The creature's unsanitary habits distressed him, and at first he thought he hated it. "I am strongly tempted of the Evil One to murder him privately; and I wish with all my heart that Mrs. Peters would drown him." But she did not, and as time went on, Bunny developed "very pleasant little ways, and a character well worth studying. . . . He has a great deal of curiosity, and an investigating disposition, and is very observant of what is going on around him." "One finds himself getting rather attached to the gentle little beast." Bunny was given away, then reclaimed because Hawthorne feared he was not being treated well. In the contest between man and rabbit, the latter emerged an easy victor.

In Concord in 1844 Hawthorne kept house for a time with a dog named Leo, for whom he fried pouts and eels, since he would not eat them raw. It troubled him to give the creature food fit for Christians, "though, for that matter, he appears to be as good a Christian as most laymen, or even some of the clergy." Leo followed Hawthorne everywhere except when he went down cellar; then he sat at the head of the stairs and howled. One Sunday morning man and dog "attended divine service . . . in a temple not made with hands," lying under an oak on the edge of a meadow.

At heart, however, Hawthorne was not a dog man but a cat man; "a dear lover of that comfortable beast," he calls himself. During a childhood illness he once knitted a pair of stockings for his cat. "How does the kitten do?" he wrote his mother in Raymond from Salem in 1820. "I hope you have not condemned her to the same fate that you did her unhappy Mother." The Hawthornes do not seem to have been models in taking care of their cats, however. When they removed from Lenox they left five behind them, who ran after the wagon for a quarter of a mile, then sat down in a row on the highest point in the road and watched them until they were out of sight. Even at the Old Manse, Pigwiggen, surely an unenterprising cat in the rich Concord meadows, nearly starved while they were absent in Salem:

When we returned from Salem we found Pigwiggen almost starved, and very melancholy. She had quite lost her playfulness; and with my usual tenderness of heart, I was inclined to end all her ills by drowning her. However, we determined first to try the efficacy of feeding her well and making her comfortable; and it has succeeded wonderfully well. She is now quite fat, and of admirable behavior. The other morning, she jumped with all four of her feet upon a hot stove. A huge caterwauling ensued, as you may suppose; but she seems to have suffered no material damage.

The affection, however, remained, and one of Hawthorne's very last characters was the spoiled kitty of "The Dolliver Romance," who sits on the doctor's shoulder while he eats trying to intercept his food between plate and mouth and even jumps upon the breakfast table and eats out of Pansie's bowl.

II

Hawthorne was never taken in by any Rousseauistic nonsense about man's natural goodness, yet he liked to think gently of "the kindly race of man." "Unless people are more than commonly disagreeable," he says, "it is my foolish habit to contract a kindness for them." We do not ordinarily think of Keats as a cynic yet Keats said, "Whatever people on the other side of the question may advance, they cannot deny that they are always surprised at hearing of a good action, and never of a bad one." But hear Hawthorne:

It is the hardest thing in the world for a noble nature—the hardest and the most shocking—to be convinced that a fellow being is going to do a wrong thing, and the consciousness of one's own inviolability renders it still more difficult to believe that one's self is to be the object of the wrong.

He tried not to allow personal idiosyncrasies to stand in the way of a fair judgment, as with Martin Farquhar Tupper, who was "the ass of asses" but also "a patient, tender, Christian man," with "an aspect of pathos and heroic endurance about him." He liked to think well of people he read about. A specimen of embroidery executed by Mary Queen of Scots prompts the reflection that "there can hardly be many more precious relics than this, in the world," and Sterne's portrait caused him to feel the need of a new biography of a writer "whose character the world has always treated with singular harshness, considering how much it owes him." As we shall see, Hawthorne was much less fussy about physical nakedness than he is sometimes given credit for having been, but the thought of stripping a fellow creature spiritually naked was unspeakably horrible to him, and he was always a bit doubtful, consequently, about satire and satirists.[2] "There can be no outrage, methinks, against our common nature," we read in *The Scarlet Letter*—"whatever the delinquencies of the individual—no outrage more flagrant than to forbid the culprit to hide his face for shame." And there is an equally moving example of Hawthorne's sensitiveness in a comment in his Italian notebooks: "It is not easy to forgive Trelawney for uncovering dead Byron's legs, and telling that terrible story about them—equally disgraceful to himself, be it truth or lie."

He was not afraid to feel tenderness and to express it frankly. "An aged man of nineteen years," he read on the gravestone of Nathaniel Mather. "It affected me deeply, when I had cleared away the grass from the half-buried stone, and read the name." In another passage he records the story of a child lost in the woods long ago. "The little boy's parents, and his brothers and sisters, who probably lived to maturity or old age, are all forgotten," he says; "but he lives in tradition, and still causes wet eyes to strangers—as he did to me." He admired the English friends of Francis Bennoch, who shed tears for him in his financial difficulties. "This is the true way to do; a man ought not to be too proud to let his eyes be moistened in the presence of God and a friend." And he marveled at Thackeray's being able to read the end of *The Newcomes* aloud without breaking down.

But he did not satisfy himself by shedding tears. His financial benefactions are described elsewhere in this volume, and he did not satisfy himself by giving money either. He maintained his own rights scrupulously, and if he unwittingly infringed those of others he owned his error frankly and without cringing. Once when he was asked why he had replied courteously to the salutation of a toper, he replied, "I would not have a drunken man politer than I."

When Hawthorne had political influence he used it; neither did he fail to bring the work of writers and artists in whom he believed to the favorable attention of publishers. But what is more impressive is his concern for the broken crocks for whom nobody else cared:

If you get the Collectorship, I charge you to do something for this miserable, God-forgotten cripple! Let it be the first thing you do, and . . . perhaps God may set it off against many wicked acts of policy that you will hereafter do, and so grant a blessing to your administration.

At Brook Farm he sat up till long past midnight with "poor Mr. Farley," who was "quite out of his wits," and later, when Sophia was absent from the Old Manse, Farley stayed there and cooked for him. "And there is really a contentment in being able to make the poor, world-worn, hopeless, half-crazy man so entirely comfortable as he seems to be here." In the custom house he was always out on the wharf at the earliest possible hour, in all kinds of weather, simply because he knew that the wages of the wharf laborers depended upon the number of hours they put in each day, and he could not hold them up.

Both Melville and Longfellow were impressed by what Melville called the "omnipresent love" expressed in Hawthorne's tales, and one of his most recent critics has remarked that he habitually "condemned actions and attitudes rather than people." At the close of *The Scarlet Letter* he even suggests that Chillingworth himself may have found salvation. Hawthorne would have understood the mood of Galsworthy's *Escape;* when his house was robbed in England he came very close to being sorry to see the robbers caught. It is no wonder that some readers have misinterpreted his point of view to the extent of supposing that Hawthorne meant to justify sin itself. But they are wrong, and his daughter Rose was right when she remembered his "religious . . . Christ-like choice of mental companionship (pity) with the greatest of all mourners, those who have sinned." From the publication of *The Scarlet Letter* on, "secret criminals of all kinds came . . . for counsel and relief" to this intensely reserved man whom many thought so inaccessible, and every confidence reposed in him was held as sacred as if he had been a priest. In spite of their own testimony, he could not even bear the thought that the twenty-seven monks who "manifested" during one of D. D. Home's seances at Hiram Powers's house in Florence were really damned. "They cannot be wholly lost, because their desire for communication with mortals shows that they need sympathy —therefore are not altogether hardened—therefore, with loving treatment, may be restored."

To be sure, Hawthorne could also denounce human beings. In this mood, Rose makes him sound much like Mark Twain:

He tore them up in passing destruction, as he always did a pond's surface with a furious pebble, as a safety-valve for his passionate determination. He talked in such fumes with an expostulatory tone, utterly devoid of ill nature; but his words purported to be the outcome of deadly hatred, as a wild creature plays with its young in imitation of a destroyer, teeth arrayed, and paw frightfully extended. Rapidly and volubly he rated the dilatory bore or flabby authoress, comfit-hearted poet or unspeakably thievish autograph fiend, in words so witty that my mother rang out her loveliest laugh, half hiding her delighted face, and the eyes that blazed with bird-like sport, in order that her husband would not notice the success he had already achieved in amusing her, and therefore cease the effort.

He could be harsh in his comments on classes too—politicians, for example—and he was as violent against the Shakers as Dickens was, and for the same reason, because it seemed to him that they were stupidly turning their backs upon everything that makes life worth living. But only in his resentment against those whose lies deprived him of his office in the custom house was there anything personal about this or any expression of a desire for revenge. Some of this last found its way into "The Custom House" sketch in *The Scarlet Letter* and left lacerations in Salem which it took long years to heal, and the utterances in private letters are considerably franker and more violent.[3]

Hawthorne lived in an age when racial problems concerned the average thinking man considerably less than they do today. Having passed through the Ethnographical rooms at the British Museum, he remarked blandly that "I care little for the varieties of the human race,—all that is really important and interesting being found in our own variety." But this is saved from offensiveness when he immediately adds, "Perhaps equally in any other."

His conscience was troubled by the white man's treatment of the red man, and he went out of his way to teach the young readers of *Grandfather's Chair* that the life of an Indian is precious in the sight of God. Few passages in Hawthorne can equal in bitterness his denunciation of the Indian killer Mrs. Duston, whom Cotton Mather had praised. If he seems less sensitive to the wrongs of the Negro, this is part of his attitude toward politics and reform in general and does not reflect any dislike of the race as such.

There are, however, two quite dreadful passages about Jews, one in *The Marble Faun*, where thousands of Jews are crowded together in the Roman ghetto "and lead a close, unclean, and multitudinous life, resembling that of maggots when they over-populate a decaying cheese," and the other a description of the beautiful Jewess whom he saw at a banquet in London and who probably colored his portrait of Miriam:

I should never have thought of touching her [he says], nor desired to touch her [since there was no occasion for his touching her, and he had not been invited to do so, his declination is in itself offensive]; for, whether owing to distinctiveness of race, my sense that she was a Jewess, or whatever else, I felt a sort of repugnance, simultaneously with my perception that she was an admirable creature.

From here he goes on to a description of her husband, "the very Jew of Jews; the distilled essence of all the Jews that have been born since Jacob's time." And he adds, "I rejoiced extremely in this Shylock, this Iscariot; for the sight of him justified me in the repugnance I have always felt towards his race." Surely there is nothing to say about this except that it belongs with Hawthorne's remarks about Margaret Fuller and about English women as demonstrating that even the best and most sensitive of men can sometimes be very insensitive indeed.

III

It may seem strange that such a man as has here been described should so often have been presented as the most solitary of American writers. *Hawthorne: A Study in Solitude*

—such is the title of one popular book about him, and there are many others in which the emphasis upon his isolation is nearly as great. Lowell thought him "rather a denizen than a citizen of what men call the world," and Newton Arvin called him an "outsider" long before Colin Wilson had popularized that term. His isolation has been psychologized into a defensive reaction to his family's decline in the world and attributed to his spending his youth in an overfeminized family circle. Franklin Pierce thought it had its origin "in a high and honorable pride," and he himself speaks of having been kept home from church and social gatherings alike by the want of proper clothes.

The legends which have developed around Hawthorne's solitude have been based upon his own testimony. Of the years following his graduation from Bowdoin he wrote, "I had always a natural tendency . . . toward seclusion; and this I now indulged to the utmost, so that for months together, I scarcely held human intercourse outside of my own family; seldom going out except at twilight, or only to take the nearest way to the most convenient solitude, which was oftenest the seashore." "I have made a captive of myself and put me in a dungeon," he told Longfellow, "and now I cannot find the key to let myself out; and if the door were open, I should be almost afraid to come out." In the dedicatory letter to Horatio Bridge, prefixed to *The Snow Image*, he proclaimed this solitude to the world: "I sat down by the wayside of life, like a man under enchantment, and a shrubbery sprang up around me, and the bushes grew to be saplings, and the saplings became trees, until no exit appeared possible, through the entangling depths of my obscurity."

As a result of this way of life, Hawthorne came to feel himself out of touch with the world, and though he knew that it had helped him to retain "the dew of my youth and the freshness of my heart," he was well aware that, being neither a scholar nor a devotee, he had not, even as a writer, derived really adequate rewards from it. "For the last ten years I have not lived, but only dreamed of living." "If I could only make tables, I should feel myself more of a man." "I'm a doomed man, and over I must go."

From such a fate Sophia Peabody saved him:

> I used to think I could imagine all passions, all feelings, and all states of the heart and mind; but how little did I know! . . . Indeed, we are but shadows; we are not endowed with real life, and all that seems most real about it is but the thinnest substance of a dream —till the heart be touched.

In the established legend this solitude swallows up Madame Hawthorne and her two daughters also, each member of the household eating in his own room and rarely holding any communication with the others. Upon her husband's death, the mother retires into a kind of living suttee, from which she never emerges in this life. With an assumption of godlike superiority unsurpassed by the worst of Hawthorne's own monstrous egotists, one biographer even passes judgment upon her: "A more worthless and useless life, except that it produced Nathaniel, it is difficult to imagine"!

Fresh from such balderdash, the student of Hawthorne may well rub his eyes upon encountering the portrait of Madame Hawthorne, as drawn by her niece Rebecca Manning:

> I remember aunt Hawthorne as busy about the house, attending to various matters. Her cooking was excellent, and she was noted for a certain kind of sauce, which nobody else knew how to make. We always enjoyed going to her when we were children, for she took great pains to please us and to give us nice things to eat. . . . In old letters and in the journal of another aunt, which has come into our possession, we read of her going about making visits, taking drives, and sometimes going on a journey. In later years she

was not well, and I do not remember that she ever came here, but her friends always received a cordial welcome when they visited her.

The legend of Madame Hawthorne's self-incarceration was set going by Julian, who got his information from his aunt Elizabeth Peabody and perhaps some of it from his mother, who knew Madame Hawthorne only in her old age. In the prime of her widowhood this descendant of Henry of Navarre ran a farm, planted fruit trees, and taught Sunday school. Hawthorne himself imputed his own taciturnity to his father, not to her. He also said she was so generous a woman that she could not help spoiling all her children. She certainly spoiled him, and however the bond between them may have weakened in later years, there can be no question that he loved her in his youth. "Why was I not a girl that I might have been pinned all my life to my mother's apron strings?" When he heard that she might give up her home in Raymond and return to Salem he was dismayed:

If you remove to Salem, I shall have no Mother to return to during the College vacations, as the expense will be too great for me to come to Salem. If you remain where you are, think how delightfully the time will pass with all your children around you, shut out from the world and nothing to disturb us. It will be a second Garden of Eden.

She was as free from moral and religious cant as her son himself, and his boyish letters to her are both impudent and affectionate, with no trace of the awe which parents of those days are supposed to have inspired in their children. When he was in trouble at college he reported his delinquencies to her honestly but with far more independence than he was reasonably entitled to show under the circumstances. Even Elizabeth Peabody says of her that she "always looked as if she had walked out of an old picture, with her antique costume

and a face of lovely sensibility and brightness; for she did not
seem at all a victim of morbid sensibility." [4]

Hawthorne's boyhood seems to have been "normal" enough.
He was never an athlete, but it is clear that he could have been
one if he had cared to take the trouble, for he was very strong
and had excellent co-ordination. Of course sports do not necessarily involve sociability, and neither do walking tours. The
forests of Maine, where Hawthorne came closest to being a
sportsman, have even sometimes been given credit for having
helped to develop the hermit in him. But his sister Louisa later
liked to recall her fishing trips with him, and we know that his
summer walking tours, which covered a good part of the
Northeast, involved many contacts with friends and stranger.
"I talk to everybody," he says.

The Bowdoin area afforded almost as rich resources for
sportsmen as Raymond itself,

gathering blueberries, in study-hours, under those tall academic
pines; or watching the great logs, as they tumbled along the current
of the Androscoggin; or shooting pigeons and gray squirrels in the
woods; or bat-fowling in the summer twilight; or catching trouts
in that shadowy little stream.

And though some sports can be practiced in solitude, games
cannot. Discipline for card-playing was an important part of
Hawthorne's trouble in college. He played, too, in Salem, with
the future mayor David Roberts, and the finally disreputable
clergyman Horace Conolly, foster son (gossips sometimes left
out the "foster") of Hawthorne's second cousin, Susan Inger-
soll, who inhabited the house on Turner Street now known as
the House of the Seven Gables. At one time Louisa seems also
to have played, and there was some whist, with the family
and others, in later life. But it is dancing that is most relevant
here, not merely Hawthorne's having been sent to dancing
school—for that has happened to many unsociable boys—but,

much more, his actually having written to Uncle Robert, when he was fourteen, "I think I had rather go to dancing school a little longer before I come to Raymond." The juvenile "Spectator," which Miss Chandler has printed, and the later (1830-31) letters to John S. Dike, printed by Mr. Hungerford, show that, at both the periods indicated, Hawthorne was completely wide-awake, with a keen interest in what was going on in the world about him.[5]

What Hawthorne believed about isolated people is not debatable. He had made up his mind as a child, when he wrote the essay "On Solitude" in "The Spectator," and he never thereafter changed:

Man is naturally a sociable being; not formed for himself alone, but destined to bear a part in the great scheme of nature. All his pleasures are heightened, and all his griefs are lessened, by participation. It is only in Society that the full energy of his mind is aroused, and all its powers drawn forth.

The tone is just the same here as in "The Prophetic Pictures": "Unless there be those around him by whose example he may regulate himself, his thoughts, desires, and hopes will become extravagant, and he the semblance, perhaps the reality of a madman." It had not changed when he wrote *Septimius Felton*. "The Christmas Banquet" is Hawthorne's "Beast in the Jungle"; it was Gervayse Hastings' tragedy that he never suffered because he had no heart to feel anything with.[6]

It is not only Hawthorne's monsters—his Rappaccinis, his Chillingworths, his Lady Eleanores, his Ethan Brands—who illustrate his feelings on this point. Even Clifford and Hepzibah Pyncheon, who are less guilty than unfortunate, and whom we are expected to like and to pity, have become half-lunatic by their exclusion from society, and Hester Prynne herself nearly incurs damnation. The narrator of "A Virtuoso's Collection" shudders at the Iron Mask—"my heart grew sick at the sight of this dreadful relic, which had shut out a human being from sympathy with his race"—and the young couple in "The Great Carbuncle" are not, in their creator's eyes, far wrong when they reject even superior insight: "never again will we desire more light than all the world may share with us." Hawthorne's feelings in this matter are revealed even in the myths. How suggestive is his account of Bellerophon's capture of Pegasus in *A Wonder Book:* "But when Bellerophon patted his head, and spoke a few authoritative, yet kind and soothing words, another look came into the eyes of Pegasus; for he was glad at heart, after so many lonely centuries, to have found a companion and a master."

All this shows Hawthorne's understanding of the dangers of living apart but of course it does not prove that he was in no danger of incurring such dangers. A man does not take out an insurance policy against going crazy simply by entering on psychiatric practice. And theoretically it is quite possible that Hawthorne warned us so sternly of the dangers of isolation because he knew them in his own experience.[7]

He himself never admitted that he had tried to work out personal problems in a tale. "When people think I am pouring myself out . . . I am merely telling what is common to human nature." Lathrop, Woodberry, and Henry James all seem to agree with this, and James reminds us that the "duskiest flowers of his invention sprang straight from the soil of his happiest days," and refers us to the notebooks to prove Hawthorne's "serenity and amenity of mind." But before we can make up our minds about this, it will be necessary to look at Hawthorne's relations with his fellows from the time of his marriage on. We shall not find testimony entirely unanimous by any means, but the conflicts which appear can, I believe, be resolved.

The life of the Hawthornes at the Old Manse has been represented as both reasonably social and as uncommonly isolated; it all depends upon what your own standards and social proclivities are. On the one hand, he will say that he did not feel really established in his new estate until the first callers came; again, Frank Stearns quotes him as saying, "George Prescott sometimes enters our paradise to bring us the products of the soil, but for weeks the snow in our avenue has been untrodden by any other guest." The truth is that the Hawthornes had a reasonable number of calls from the literati of Concord and others but they were also left a good deal to themselves. But surely this itself is "normal" for a honeymooning couple. Adam and Eve had but one visitor in Eden, and he got them expelled from it.

They must have had less company in Salem, since in November 1846 Sophia wrote her mother that they had spent their first evening away from home since Una's birth almost three years before. Yet Hawthorne somewhat amazingly became an officer of the Salem Lyceum, and his invitation to Emerson to lecture there does not reflect either shyness or coldness toward Emerson personally:

I wish . . . for myself and wife, to prefer our claim, as townspeople of your own, to receive you under our roof. Sophia is particularly desirous of showing you our children; and, for my part, I shall be truly glad to see you on that and many other accounts.

Lenox marked the high-water point of the Hawthorne social activity before they went abroad. "It is very singular," said Sophia, "how much more we are in the center of society in Lenox than we were in Salem." Fields has written a detailed description of Hawthorne's gaiety upon one particular occasion.[8] It is unmistakably the account of a man who is at last beginning to feel at home in the world.

One would not think of him as at home in England, yet in a sense he was, for as the representative of his country he carried his home with him. People came to him, as a lion or a government official or both; he did not have to make any advances. When they did not come, he let them alone, never seeking out English writers, for example, though by this time he was well enough known so that they would certainly have welcomed him. But those who did come he received cordially, and though he sometimes got tired of them, he handled them well. "I have received, and been civil to, at least 10,000 visitors since I came to England," he says, "and I never wish to be civil to anybody again." Yet H. F. Chorley, who judged him "genial and not over sensitive," said he had a heartier laugh than any man of his acquaintance except Carlyle, and Moncure D. Conway writes, "You had only to mention the name of Hawthorne in houses he had entered throughout Europe, and every face beamed with sunshine." He himself boasts to Sophia about how he carried it off with the Motleys: "Thou wouldst be stricken dumb to see how quietly I accept a whole string of invitations, and what is more, perform my engagements without a murmur." And, again:

I met Miss Cushman, on Saturday, in the Strand, and she asked me to dinner, but I could not go, being already engaged to meet another actress! I have a strange run of luck as regards actresses, having made friends with the three most prominent ones since I came to London, and I find them all excellent people; and they all inquire for thee!!

The most amazing aspect of Hawthorne's life in England was the aplomb with which he carried off his obligations as a public speaker. It is true that his inability to speak in early life has been exaggerated. In college he shirked speaking whenever it was possible to do so, but we know of occasions when he did speak and apparently without agony. It is amusing to find Louisa writing their mother on his sixteenth birthday that "Nathaniel delivered a most excellent Oration this morning to no other hearers but me." [9] But certainly there had been nothing to prepare us—or him—for such a success as Fields records, on an occasion when he was required to hold forth impromptu at Brighton.

I imagined his face a deep crimson, and his hands trembling with nervous horror; but judge of my surprise, when he rose to reply with so calm a voice and so composed a manner, that, in all my experience of dinner-speaking, I never witnessed such a case of apparent ease. . . . There was no hesitation, no sign of lack of preparation, but he went on for about ten minutes in such a masterly manner, that I declare it was one of the most successful efforts of the kind ever made.

Hawthorne's own judgments of such accomplishments are more interesting than the facts themselves. His treatment of Old Stony Phiz in "The Great Stone Face" would not have led us to expect that he had any very high regard for the arts of the orator, though perhaps he is no more severely treated than the representatives of other professions. On the one hand Hawthorne tells us, "I don't in the least admire my own oratory; but I do admire my pluck in speaking at all." And again he says that anybody can do it "who will be content to talk onward without saying anything." Sometimes he did well when he expected to do badly and vice versa, and like most self-conscious men he preferred large audiences in which he could not single out individuals and wonder about their individual reactions. He admitted that sometimes the excitement stimulated him—"not exactly pleasure, but more piquant than pleasure"—and once at least he had that sense of rapport with his hearers which marks the true speaker. "Certainly there was a very kind feeling in the audience; and it is wonderful how conscious the speaker is of sympathy, and how it warms and animates him." Yet his permanent attitude toward speaking was not changed in the slightest degree. "I have no practice, in any mode of public speaking," he wrote Bryant in 1861, after his return to America, "and am often compelled (owing to this deficiency) to decline offers similar to the liberal one with which you have now honored me."

Yet Lowell and others thought Hawthorne "easier in society" after his European sojourn. So he seemed to Julia Ward Howe, recalling, by way of contrast, the day she had visited at the Old Manse, when, in response to Mrs. Hawthorne's summons, he had only shown himself in the door and then promptly bolted. Sanborn shared this impression, though he adds, rather strangely, that Hawthorne was also "less simple and agreeable in his intimate manners and general character" than he had formerly been. But he goes on to quote Thoreau as having written his sister that their fellow townsman was "as amiable and child-like as ever."

Testimony to Hawthorne's unsociability, abundant throughout his life, takes various forms. The extremest statement comes from Henry James, Sr., who, seeing him at the Saturday Club, thought that he acted like a rogue in a company of detectives. "How he buried his eyes in his plate, and ate with such a voracity that no person should dare to ask him a question!" (Years later the younger Henry James was to notice that in his journals Hawthorne called everybody "Mr.") Even in college, and despite the evidences of Hawthorne's conviviality there, Jonathan Cilley said, "I love Hawthorne; I admire him; but I do not know him. He lives in a mysterious world of thought and imagination which he never permits me to enter." "He never speaks, except in a tête-a-tête," said Longfellow, "and then not much." And Mrs. Longfellow adds that he

has a fine manly head but is the most shy and diffident of men. The freest conversation did not thaw forth more than a mono-syllable. . . . I really pity a person under this spell of reserve—he must long to utter his thoughts and feels under a magic ban upon so doing, as Dante's poor sinners could not weep through their frozen lids.

There is an amusing story of his once "ducking" with James T. Fields in the meadow grass at The Wayside to escape the eyes of a passer-by. And charming as he was to young William Dean Howells, the visitor had to admit that "there was a great deal of silence in it all, and at times, in spite of his shadowy kindness, I felt my spirits sink."

When Hawthorne came to Concord to live at the Old Manse, Margaret Fuller promised Emerson that he would "find him more *mellow* than most fruits at your board, and of distinct flavor too." She was so wrong that after Hawthorne's death Emerson found himself lamenting the "unwillingness and caprice" which had thwarted his attempts to "conquer a friendship." "It was easy to talk with him,—there were no barriers,—only, he said so little, that I talked too much, and stopped only because, as he gave no indications, I feared to exceed." [10]

Emerson's friend, Bronson Alcott, was even less successful with Hawthorne:

During all the time he lived near me . . . I seldom caught sight of him; and when I did it was to lose it the moment he suspected he was visible; oftenest seen on his hilltop screened behind the shrubbery and disappearing like a hare into the bush when surprised. I remember of his being in my house but twice, and then he was so ill at ease that he found excuse for leaving politely forthwith,—"the stove was so hot," "the clock ticked so loud." Yet he once complained to me of his wish to meet oftener, and dwelt on the delights of fellowship, regretting he had so little. . . . What neighbor of his ever caught him on the highway, or ventured to approach his threshold? . . . Yet if by chance admitted, welcome in a voice that a woman's might own for its hesitancy and tenderness; his eyes telling the rest.[11]

It should be remembered that Hawthorne was never really en rapport with Emerson—"that everlasting rejecter of all that is, and seeker for he knows not what"—and that he considered both the Alcotts bores. "It was never so well understood at The Wayside that its owner had retiring habits," writes Rose Hawthorne, "as when Alcott was reported to be approaching." Sophia's eyes "changed to a darker gray at his advents, as they did only when she was silently asserting herself." Once he read to the Hawthornes a "particularly long poem" of his own composition, "a seemingly harmless thing, from which they never recovered." Nevertheless, Hawthorne considered Alcott to possess a saintly character, which was more than he believed about Mrs. Alcott, for he once told her husband to his face that it was quite impossible for any neighbor to live on amicable terms with her, and Alcott agreed! One night, after Emerson and Alcott had departed from The Wayside, Hawthorne pulled out his watch and remarked to Gail Hamilton, "Only half-past nine, and we have been through all this siege."

There are many stories about Hawthorne's reserve in social gatherings. The most famous one relates to an occasion in Concord when he

sat upon the edge of the circle, a little withdrawn, his head slightly thrown forward upon his breast, and his bright eyes clearly burning under his black brow. . . . He rose and walked to the window, and stood quietly there for a long time, watching the dead white landscape. No appeal was made to him, nobody looked after him, the conversation flowed steadily on as if every one understood that his silence was to be respected. It was the same thing at table. In vain the silent man imbibed aesthetic tea. Whatever fancies it inspired did not flower at his lips. But there was a light in his eye which assured me that nothing was lost. . . . When he presently rose and went, Emerson, with the "slow, wise smile" that breaks over his face, like day over the sky, said:

"Hawthorne rides well his horse of the night."

H. T. Tuckermann, similarly, describes him in London as seating himself "noiselessly" by the table, and bending over a magazine "with a kind of subdued content . . . like a man who could fold an author's thoughts up in his own with an affectionate patience."

Rebecca Harding Davis found Hawthorne even in his own house "like Banquo's ghost among the thanes at the banquet." Generally, however, he was much easier when he was in control of the situation.

I love Mr. Hawthorne very much [wrote Ada Shepard to her fiancé, while she was staying with the Hawthornes in Europe], and do not understand why people believe him cold. He is certainly extremely reserved, but he is noble and true and good, and is full of kindly feeling. . . . I admire him exceedingly, and do not feel in the least afraid of him as I had imagined I should be.

Yet it is interesting that she had expected to be. "Why do they treat me so?" Hawthorne once asked a friend. "Why, they're afraid of you" was the reply. "But I tremble at *them*," said Hawthorne. "They think," she explained, "that you're imagining all sorts of terrible things." "Heavens," he exclaimed; "if they only knew what I *do* think about."

His own view was that he was quite willing to reveal himself but that it was impossible for him to take the initiative:

I am glad to think that God sees through my heart, and, if any angel has power to penetrate into it, he is welcome to know everything that is there. Yes, and so may any mortal who is capable of full sympathy, and therefore worthy to come into my depths. But

he must find his own way there. I can neither guide nor enlighten
him.

It took an angel—or a "poor devil." He was always at home
in the grass-covered shanties of the Irish immigrants who were
working on the railroad.

I have heard people say Hawthorne was cold and distant [writes
his Negro friend of early days, William Symmes]; if he was so,
there was one of his youthful associates, who, as the world goes,
was not his equal socially, certainly not intellectually, who was
never forgotten. The last time I saw him we were at Liverpool;
he recognized me across the street, and "hove me to." We had a
long talk, and he conversed in that easy, bewitching style, of which
he was perfect master when he pleased.

With an eccentric like Delia Bacon he had the patience of
a saint; indeed he says specifically that he talked to her with
perfect ease, recognizing her as one of those "lonely people"
who are ready to "bubble over" as soon as they are assured of
a sympathetic listener. It was only the "great" whom he scruti-
nized carefully and accepted or rejected upon his own terms;
the merchants and businessmen of Salem though him so stand-
offish and even arrogant during his service in the custom house
that it has been argued that their hostility may have had something to do with his removal.[12] His conversation was hesitant;
he liked plain, out-of-the-way hotels, where he could be
entered upon the register as the "friend" of his traveling companion, with all his traces so carefully covered that nobody
could possibly follow him; he loved a secluded corner in his
publisher's office, from which he would emerge, cordially
enough, to greet an admirer, only to retire thankfully again
as soon as possible. Even Sophia recognized—and respected—
his reserve. "I never dared to gaze at him, even I," she wrote
after his death, "unless his lids were down. It seemed an in-

vasion into a holy place. To the last, he was in a measure to me a divine mystery; for he was so to himself."

She was the most important bridge between himself and the world, and they both recognized it. "I will never venture into company," he wrote her playfully in 1838, "unless I can put myself under the protection of Sophie Hawthorne. She, I am sure, will take care that no harm comes to me." But he is not playful at all but completely in earnest when he says, "I never, till now, had a friend who could give me repose;—all have disturbed me; and whether for pleasure or pain, it was still disturbance, but peace overflows from your heart into mine." Nine years later, when he had been married to her six years, the tone is the same but much more tender: "Other people have occasionally been more or less agreeable; but I think I was always more at ease alone than in anybody's company, till I knew thee. And now I am only myself when thou art within my reach. Thou art an unspeakably beloved woman." "My wife," he once confided to his journal, "is, in the strictest sense, my sole companion, and I need no other."

The question arises, then: Did Sophia draw Hawthorne out of his solitude, or did he draw her into it? Naturally, since these people had achieved a real marriage, both these things happened. Sophia herself was no society maiden, and she was intelligent enough to realize that at thirty-eight her husband was too old to have his way of life completely revolutionized. "You know that he has but just stepped over the threshold of a hermitage. He is just *not* a hermit still." He always realized that he might "relapse" without her, and once, when they were separated, he resolved (though he was not able to achieve it), that he would be completely silent while she was away! Late in life he wrote that he had never "really talked" with half-a-dozen human beings.

But are there many sensitive, highly developed persons who

have done much better than this? Of course Hawthorne's standards in this matter were not those of the average man —or still more, the average woman—who would rather talk with somebody he hates than not talk at all. Human beings were the inexhaustible focus of his interest, and few such curious observers have studied them with more sympathy. Nevertheless—or perhaps therefore—he also felt the need of viewing them from a station somewhat removed. Hawthorne loved crowds—a man can always lose himself in a crowd—but he knew that even a procession is unimpressive if the spectator is too close to it.[13] "My father fostered his interest in human nature," wrote his daughter Rose, "by regarding it instead of embracing it." He needed society but, like Coverdale in *Blithedale*, he must withdraw from it periodically to save the better part of himself. "The real Me was never an associate of the community," he wrote of the Brook Farm sojourn, and he might have said the same of many other activities. Even as a child he told his sisters stories of wonderful journeys he contemplated making, all ending with the same refrain, "And I'll never come back again!" Harry Levin comments on his tendency as narrator to place himself at an "esthetic distance" from his subject; he often becomes the spiritualized Paul Pry he once expressed a desire to be. Like Henry James, and unlike the often close and embarrassingly intimate writers of today, he keeps what E. E. Stoll once described as "the cool, serene distance of art."

When Delia Bacon told Hawthorne about her difficulty in meeting people he replied, "I can entirely sympathize with you in your reluctance; none better than I. To tell you the truth, though I see people by scores, every day, I still shrink from any interview of which I am forewarned." I am sure that this was true but still I do not think Hawthorne was "shy" by any proper definition of that term. At Brook Farm, in the custom house, in his consulship, he did whatever needed to be done and did it conscientiously and efficiently. He visited prisons, hospitals, lunatic asylums, workhouses. He never shrank from the contacts involved in doing whatever had to be done to carry out an obligation whose hold upon him he recognized and acknowledged. This would not, I think, have been possible for a "shy" man. Moreover, he often found that he "liked" the people with whom such duties brought him into contact. But as soon as the job was done and the call of duty satisfied, he withdrew from all such activities again.

In other words, insofar as Hawthorne was solitary, it was not because he shrank from contacts with human beings or could not manage them but because he preferred to be alone. This is not shyness; it is an extreme fastidiousness and sensitiveness. In his human relations Hawthorne was not a gourmand but an epicure. He enjoyed contacts with humanity upon his own terms, and when they ceased to be rewarding he dropped them.

V

In one aspect, Hawthorne's kindness and friendliness has never been questioned: he was unfailingly generous with his money. Even back in the 'forties, when he was almost a pauper himself, he wrote:

I have a liking for vagrants of all sorts, and never, that I know of, refused my mite to a wandering beggar, when I had anything in my own pocket. There is so much wretchedness in the world, that we may safely take the word of any mortal when they say that they need our assistance; and even should we be deceived, still the good to ourselves resulting from a kind act, is worth more than the trifle by which we purchase it.

When he got to Liverpool he was appealed to on a whole-sale scale, and every impecunious American in England steered straight for the consulate. Now it was a deranged young man whose medical expenses must be paid; again there was a sea captain who had died at his boarding house and had to be buried. It is true that Hawthorne sometimes conducted an investigation of those who appealed to him, but the terms of the investigation were likely to be "rigged" in favor of the applicant. Simultaneously he was keeping up his benevolences in America. In 1854 he risked $2000 of his own money to supply food and clothing for the troops who had been wrecked with the *San Francisco*, the government having neglected to provide for them and the American ambassador Buchanan assuming a *laissez-faire* attitude.

Among the objects of Hawthorne's benevolence in England, his countrywoman Delia Bacon, the mother of the Baconian theory, received by far the greatest attention. He admired *The Philosophy of the Plays of Shakespeare Expounded* (1857), oddly enough, not because he shared Miss Bacon's contempt for the "Stratford Player" but because he did not; her appreciation of the greatness of the plays, despite her heresy concerning their authorship, was so penetrating, he believed, that her book would show Shakespeare an even greater writer than he had ever appeared before. He arranged for the publication of the volume, therefore, on both sides of the Atlantic, and risked—and lost—$1000 on the printing of it, and it was not all for the glory of Shakespeare; much of it was pure, unselfish pity for a brilliant but unstable woman who was rapidly approaching a final crack-up. He admitted he "would rather that Providence had employed some other instrument," but since it had not, and since Miss Bacon "must be kept alive," it seemed to him there was only one thing to do. "You say nothing about the state of your funds," he writes in one letter to her. "Pardon me for alluding to the subject; but you promised to apply to me in case of need. I am ready." When she broke at last he made himself responsible for her care and kept in touch with her until he left England; at one time he had even arranged for her return to America. Of course she turned against him in spite of all his kindness; indeed she nearly refused to permit the book to be published after it had been printed, so incensed was she over his failure to avow himself a Baconian and her disciple in the Preface he wrote for her. Disgustedly he vowed that "this shall be the last of my benevolent follies, and I will never be kind to anybody again as long as I live."

But the leopard did not change his spots, neither then nor after his return to America. Late in 1860 he wrote Ticknor from Concord asking him to pay a friend $50: "It is impossible not to assist an old acquaintance in distress—for once, at least." And he adds a P.S.: "Do not write to me about this; for I do not wish my wife to know how I throw away my money."

He needed "a great deal of money" now. "I wonder how people manage to live economically." He didn't expect to get it; instead he expected to die in the poor house. Julian's college bills were enormous, and taxes were twice as high in 1863 as they had been in 1862. Once, while he was in England, he had flirted with the idea of selling The Wayside and buying Alcott's Orchard House nearby, but this had not worked out, and The Wayside had been rebuilt and enlarged, which had made life a burden for months and cost four times the estimate. "What will be the use of having a house, if it costs me all my means of living in it?" He drove himself to produce a new romance, meanwhile throwing off Our Old Home as a financial stopgap.

Hawthorne certainly had greater financial security at the end than he had ever had before, but he did not worry about money less. When he died in 1864 the estate was appraised at $28,034.61, of which one-third was paid to Mrs. Hawthorne, plus two-thirds of the balance as guardian for Julian and Rose, the other third going directly to the only child who was of age, Una.

VI

The worst handicap a man can have in his relations with others is an excessive regard for himself. Hawthorne is not usually thought of as a self-assertive person or as one who thought of himself more highly than he ought to think. He made almost a religion out of his unwillingness to exercise power over other human beings. His self-portrait at the beginning of "Rappaccini's Daughter" is modest though perhaps a bit coy, and he is considerably more coy when he permits the children in *A Wonder Book* to speculate about "our neighbor in the red house." All his life he experienced a recurrent dream in which he saw himself still at school, unable to get out into the world and make a success of himself as his contemporaries had done. "How strange that it should come now," he writes in 1855, "when I may call myself famous, and prosperous! —when I am happy, too!" He had a reasonable but certainly not excessive interest in portraits and photographs. Perhaps his most considered self-judgment was made in a letter to Delia Bacon:

. . . you will find me always just the same as I have been; and if ever I seem otherwise, the fault is in the eyes that look at me. Nor do I pretend to be very good; there are hundreds of kinder and better people in the world; but such as I am, I am genuine, and in keeping with myself.

In *Our Old Home* Hawthorne makes the amazing statement that he had never heard his own voice at declamatory pitch before he was dragooned into public speaking in England. Even if this is not literally true we are still obviously dealing with a man of very unusual self-control. But "control" is the key-word, not "weakness." Even as a boy Hawthorne refused to endure bantering and was prepared to fight if necessary rather than submit to it. "I am sixteen years old," he wrote his mother in 1820. "In five years I shall belong to myself." His sister says that his family was "almost absolutely obedient to him" in the days of his literary apprenticeship. The man who began a campaign biography with the statement that "this species of writing is too remote from his customary occupations—and, he may add, from his tastes—to be very satisfactorily done, without more time and practice than he would be willing to expend for such a purpose" was not likely to be pushed around by anybody. Both stevedores and sea captains learned this when he was inspector of customs. George Lathrop says that in his later life "rude people jostling him in a crowd would give way at once 'at the sound of his low and almost irresolute voice.' "[14]

When Margaret Fuller tactlessly suggested that Ellery Channing and her sister, his wife, might be received as boarders at the Old Manse, Sophia would probably have yielded rather than say no, but Hawthorne rejected the suggestion with perfect tact and firmness. "Had it been proposed to Adam and Eve to receive two angels into their Paradise, as *boarders*, I doubt whether they would have been altogether pleased to consent." He was quite as firm in a more difficult situation at Lenox when a difference of opinion arose as to the ownership of the fruit at the house they had rented. "I infinitely prefer a small right to a great favor," he wrote Mrs. Tappan. And having established his own conviction of his right to the fruit quite uncompromisingly, he ended: "But would it not be wiser to drop the question of right, and receive it as a free-will offering from us?"

Frank P. Stearns quotes Bronson Alcott as saying that there was only one will in Hawthorne's family, and that was Hawthorne's will. Alcott may not have been the best judge, but Rose Hawthorne reinforces him when she writes, "Everything that was done was done first and best for him." Rose was not complaining. Mrs. Hawthorne regarded her husband as a god, and she seems to have communicated this point of view to her children. Even after his death she felt "like veiling myself" when she read over his letters. "Why am I not already transfigured into a Shining One by such a love, so expressed?" I am raising no question here concerning Hawthorne's deserving such devotion. But the fact that it existed made it inevitable that he should exist in a certain atmosphere of adulation.

Apparently Hawthorne would have agreed with Sarah Bernhardt that human beings "ought to hate very rarely, as it is too fatiguing, remain indifferent a great deal, forgive often, and never forget." He was often annoyed but he seems to have cherished real resentment only against the Reverend Charles W. Upham and his allies, who forced him out of his position at Salem. Upham himself he may have caricatured as Judge Pyncheon.[15] In a vitriolic letter to Longfellow, written before he knew whether his enemies would be successful or not, Hawthorne glorified his proposed revenge by making himself the avenging champion of literature itself and approached arrogance as closely as he ever came:

If they will pay no reverence to the imaginative power when it causes herbs of grace and sweet-scented flowers to spring up along their pathway, then they should be taught what it can do in the way of producing nettles, skunk-cabbage, deadly night-shade, wolf's bane, dog-wood. If they will not be grateful for its works of beauty and beneficence, then let them dread it as a pervasive and penetrating mischief, that can reach them at their firesides and in their bed-chambers, follow them to far countries, and make their very graves refuse to hide them.

Longfellow must have smiled.

Did Hawthorne, then, lack humor? There is no doubt that he was capable of both creating and relishing amusement. But he lacked the detachment of the true comic spirit. "The Celestial Railroad," the most successful of his humorous works, does not misrepresent him; it is sarcastic, even mildly sardonic; in a sense it is one of the most earnest things he ever wrote. Trollope found "a weird, mocking spirit" everywhere in Hawthorne's work, with no page untinged by satire. It is not surprising that there should have been a suggestion of mockery even in his smile.

This mockery had already appeared in the childish "Spectator," as when he has his Aunt Mary, "YOUNG, being under FIFTY years of age, and of GREAT BEAUTY," advertise for a husband under seventy, and possessed of ten thousand dollars. He could be sharp, as when, in England, he was informed that Fields was not coming over until next year, being afraid of seasickness: "Does he expect immunity from seasickness next year? Or are we to have a railway across?" The "little odd volumes" in Dr. Ripley's library at the Old Manse impressed him "as if they had been intended for very large ones, but had been blighted in an early stage of their growth, and so were stunted and withered"—surely a Dickensian touch.

Even with his children, Hawthorne, though charmingly fanciful, does not seem to have been really gay.

We were introduced to General Crook [he writes Julian, while off on his trip to Washington and its environs in 1862], who showed us his fortress and drew out his troops for our inspection, though I have an idea that he would have resisted our authority, had he dared; but in that case, I should have had him immediately shot.

And certainly his spirit of mockery did not stop short at himself. For all his raptures about his marriage, he could write Louisa:

The execution took place yesterday. We made a Christian end, and came straight to Paradise, where we abide at the present writing. We are as happy as people can be, without making themselves ridiculous, and might be even happier; but, as a matter of taste, we choose to stop short at this point.

He added that he intended "to improve vastly by marriage —that is, if I can find room for improvement." "I am glad you have got rid of so many of the new books," he tells Ticknor, after he has made his success. "Sweep them off as fast as you can. Don't let your shelves be disgraced with such trash." And when, at the bitter end, he cannot finish his novel for love or for money, the tone is the same, and he suggests two forms of announcement for the *Atlantic:*

We are sorry to hear (but know not whether the public will share our grief) that Mr. Hawthorne is out of health and is thereby prevented, for the present, from producing another of his promised (or threatened) Romances, intended for this magazine.

Mr. Hawthorne's brain is addled at last, and, much to our satisfaction, he tells us that he cannot possibly go on with the Romance announced on the cover of the January Magazine. We consider him finally shelved, and shall take early occasion to bury him under a heavy article, carefully summing up his merits (such as they were) and his demerits, what few of them can be touched upon in our limited space.

For some people social life is complicated by their attitude toward currently popular indulgences. Drinking, smoking, and gaming (of which last we hear nothing thereafter) were all a part of Hawthorne's life in college, though when he became a senior he apparently reformed.[16] "I have not played at all this term," he wrote his mother in the spring of 1822, after his one serious brush with presidential authority. "I have not drank any kind of spirits or wine this term, and shall not till the last week." That this resolution was kept we may judge from another letter to his sister in August:

I have involved myself in no "foolish scrape," as you say all my friends suppose; but ever since my misfortune I have been as steady as a signpost, and as sober as a deacon, have been in no "blows" this term, nor drank any kind of "wine or strong drink." So that your comparison of me to the "prodigious son" will hold good in nothing, except that I shall probably return penniless, for I have had no money this six weeks.

Later in life, Hawthorne's enemies sometimes accused him of drinking immoderately. Such charges always made his friends indignant, though Sanborn quotes Dr. G. B. Loring as saying that Hawthorne "could eat more and drink more than any man he ever dined with." Sanborn himself adds that Hawthorne had no "uncontrolled appetites." Horatio Bridge, speaking of the college years, says that "he rarely exceeded the bounds of moderation," and the qualifying force of the adverb is reinforced when he adds that Hawthorne "could drink a great deal of wine without, apparently, being affected by it." Defending him against the charge of intemperance in England, Francis Bennoch says similarly that "he had a head of iron."

Though I do not see how he could have found out this much without testing it, I do not believe that Hawthorne was ever in danger of becoming a drunkard. It must be admitted, however, that he often bears testimony against himself. There may have been a certain element of bravado in this. Thus, his sittings with the painter Leutze were enjoyable because Leutze plied him with cigars and champagne—"and we quaffed and smoked yesterday, in a blessed state of mutual good-will, for three hours and a half, during which the picture made a really miraculous progress." Accepting an invitation from Lowell, he qualifies, "I shall have very great pleasure in the visit, especially if I do not drink and smoke too much at the Club dinner (as I usually do) and fill the pipe too often in your study—as I did the last time." And he likes James Buchanan better than he had expected to like him because "he takes his wine like a true man" and "loves a good cigar."

He thought gin more wholesome and agreeable than champagne, and several times ascribed his public speaking prowess in England to "pot-valor" or being "about half-seas over."

Your claret was most excellent and acceptable [he wrote Ticknor in 1852], and has already given me a great deal of comfort. Some other friends have sent me some sauterne, some champagne, and some sherry; and I have laid in a supply of first-rate brandy on my own hook; so that I hope to keep myself pretty jolly in spite of the Maine Law.

He permitted Julian to taste wine for the first time at the Monte Tastaccio in Italy. The boy drank two glasses, "and when we rose to depart I was greatly perplexed, and my father vastly tickled, to discover a lack of coherence between my legs and my intentions"—surely a choicely paternal sense of humor. During the last year of his life Hawthorne remarked that he wished to teach Julian the taste of good wine so that he might not take to the horrible punches he understood were being served at Harvard. Even at the very end, when he was too sick for any kind of indulgence, the old bravado flared in his question to the Fieldses: "Why has the good old custom of coming together to get drunk gone out? Think of the delight of drinking in pleasant company and then lying down to sleep a deep strong sleep."

Hawthorne did not think much of the English palate, but he was impressed by the quantity of potables the English got down, compared to their American cousins.

It is delightful to see how little progress tee-totalism has yet made in these parts; these respectable persons probably went away drunk, that night, yet thought none of the worse of themselves or one another for it. It is like returning to times twenty years gone by, for a New Englander to witness such simplicity of manners.

In other moods, "simplicity" did not seem quite the word for it, and he speaks of the English as "a nation of beastly eaters and beastly drinkers." Once he even plays the innocent as coyly as any stage ingenue when he writes Bennoch complaining of a headache the day after he had eaten two dinners "with wine and ale in large proportion," and going on to explain how Albert Smith had made him drink five whiskey toddies. In his "Yankee simplicity" he thought they were "some kind of teetotal beverage." To which one can only hope that the Englishman retorted, "Walker!"

There are some indications—though the evidence is not conclusive—that Hawthorne was less interested in drinking during his later years. As early as his visit to Bridge in 1837 he noted that though an abundance of "drinkables" had been provided, they were neither as thirsty as they once had been. In 1851 he thanked Pike for gin received some time since but not yet acknowledged or uncorked. In 1856 he says he no longer has any interest in liquor though he still enjoys a cigar. Late in life he told Holmes there was no point in his coming to the Saturday Club, since he could no longer either drink or eat.

There are also a good many temperance passages in Hawthorne's writings. Liquor is evil in "Ethan Brand" and in "David Swan," and the new Adam and Eve turn from it as, to be sure, they turn also from meat. The disgusting aspects of both drinking and smoking are stressed in *Dr. Grimshawe's Secret*. Neither practice is known in the Heavenly City of "The Celestial Railroad," which is one reason why the laodiceans and latitudinarians do not care to go there. In Vanity Fair "if a customer wished to renew his stock of youth, the dealers offered him a set of false teeth and an auburn wig;

if he demanded peace of mind, they recommended opium or the brandy bottle." In "A Rill from the Town Pump" liquor is linked up with every conceivable evil including war; it is not surprising that this piece should have been used as a temperance tract. Among Hawthorne's more amiable characters, only Coverdale, of *The Blithedale Romance*, is much addicted to either the bottle or the weed, but the detailed description of a luxurious Boston saloon in that novel culminates in a discussion of the cause and cure of drinking from the standpoint of "we temperance people" which seems quite out of character for Coverdale himself.

For all his dislike of interfering in other people's affairs, Hawthorne seems to have been seriously concerned about intemperance in his friends. He exerted himself in Zechariah Burchmore's behalf by exhortation, example, and by finding employment for him, and according to Julian he also once gave good advice to Pierce. But his most amusing labor in the vineyard occurred at Liverpool in 1855, when he persuaded a sea captain to sign the total abstinence pledge, and then, "on the strength of this good deed," allowed himself an extra glass or two that evening and consequently had a headache the next day.

In the paper on "English Poverty" in *Our Old Home* Hawthorne shows his awareness of the depredations wrought by gin in the London slums, and also his realization that, so long as poverty-breeding conditions were allowed to exist, cutting off gin would not alone suffice to solve the problem. He had not needed to wait until he reached London to realize this, for he had discussed the matter at some length in a long paragraph which he finally cut out of the manuscript of *The Blithedale Romance:*

Human nature, in my opinion, has a naughty instinct that approves of wine, at least, if not of stronger liquor. The temperance-men may preach till doom's day; and still this cold and barren world will look warmer, kindlier, mellower, through the medium of a toper's glass; nor can they, with all their efforts, really spill his draught upon the floor, until some hitherto unthought of discovery shall supply him with a truer element of joy. The general atmosphere of life must first be rendered so inspiriting that he will not need his delirious solace. The custom of tippling has its defensible side, as well as any other question. But these good people snatch at the old, time-honored demijohn, and offer nothing—either sensual or moral—nothing whatever to supply its place, and human life, as it goes with a multitude of men, will not endure so great a vacuum as would be left by the withdrawal of that big-bellied convexity. The space, which it now occupies, must somehow or other be filled up. As for the rich, it would be little matter if a blight fell upon their vineyards; but the poor man—whose only glimpse of a better state is through the muddy medium of his liquor—what is to be done for him? The reformers should make their efforts positive, instead of negative; they must do away with evil by substituting good.

Hawthorne first mentions tobacco in a letter he wrote to Louisa when he was sixteen, where he says that he has taken to chewing it with all his might, "which, I think, raises my spirits." He felt that tobacco smoke creates a sympathetic medium for social contacts; he liked the thought of associating it with wayside shrines in Italy; in "Mr. Higginbotham's Catastrophe" he even made New England country girls great pipe smokers. "I should be glad to smoke a cigar with him," he writes of Tennyson.

How much Hawthorne smoked is problematical. Very little, says Julian, perhaps half-a-dozen boxes of cigars in the course of his life. One box, presented by Franklin Pierce, lasted him five or six years. He "would go for months without touching a cigar or thinking of one."

Rose, on the other hand, says he smoked one cigar a day. There is an 1851 letter in which he orders 250 cigars from

Burchmore, calling this about a year's supply. On the other hand, there is a letter to Ticknor in which he promises to smoke the cigars the latter has sent him "after breakfast and dinner." Incidentally Hawthorne seems to have tended to rely largely upon gifts for both alcohol and tobacco, which is hardly the mark of a thoroughgoing addict.

According to Ada Shepard, Mrs. Hawthorne was not averse to an occasional glass of wine, but she disliked the smell of tobacco intensely (may, indeed, have been allergic to it), and one cannot but wonder what she thought about associating something so unpleasant with the man she adored. Once, during their courtship, he came to her smelling of tobacco and wrote afterwards, with typical, unregenerative, lover-like humility, that he was "glad that this vapor of tobacco smoke did, for once, roll thus darkly and densely between us, because it helps me to hate the practice forevermore. Thou wast very sweet not to scold me fiercely, for allowing myself to be so impregnated." After their marriage she seems not to have interfered with him, except that it was understood he was not to smoke in the house. When, in her absence from Lenox, he and Melville "smoked cigars even within the sacred precincts of the sitting-room," it was a sufficiently unusual circumstance to require chronicle. At another time and place, when the aforementioned Conolly—"whom I can no more keep from smoking than I could the kitchen chimney"—came into the study while he was writing a letter to her, he detailed the circumstance for fear the tobacco "might perfume this letter, and make thee think it came from thy husband's enormity."

Drinking and smoking are moral issues for many people; eating can become one only through intemperance. When Sophia Peabody first began to interest herself in the eating habits of her fiancé, he told her that, though he was willing to live on bread and water if it pleased her, left to himself his appetite was as indiscriminate as that of an ostrich. "Setting aside fat pork, I refuse no other Christian meat." In his youth, at Salem, he would come home from his winter evening walks to a pint bowl of thick chocolate crammed full of bread. "Eating never hurt him then," writes his sister, "and he liked good things." There is a charming passage on breakfast in *The House of the Seven Gables* but this is more concerned with the spiritual qualities of the meal than the sensual. In Europe he came under the spell of a handsomely set table and learned that America still had much to learn about dining as an art. He discovered that the English had much to learn from the French also, and here the ancient Puritan fear raised its head: when you eat English food, you know you are indulging yourself, but French food is so delicate that you may indulge without realizing it, a condition fraught with spiritual danger.

Hawthorne was no gourmet, and when he was left alone in the house he was always likely to go without a good meal to save the trouble of cooking it. According to Julian, the table was "almost as simple as Baucis and Philemon's," but when he particularizes he leaves the reader in some doubt whether he has actually read his father's tale. They had, says Julian,

vegetables, a leg of mutton, rice or tapioca pudding, water cool from the well. For breakfast, we had buckwheats or pandowdy, or both—tall piles of the former renewed at will and, to keep them hot, a wonderful metal platter which was an heirloom from the Pilgrims, a double-decker with hot water between decks; then, molasses from the West Indians, which poured out stiff and black as ebony. Apples, cherries, strawberries in the Lord's seasons; hot cocoa and fresh milk.

Hawthorne himself has recorded the bill of fare of a dinner served at the Tremont House in Boston in honor of Arthur Hugh Clough. There were turtle soup, baked black fish, boiled capon and Virginia ham, with macaroni, riz de veau and cauli-

flower, canvasback duck, omelette soufflé, wine jelly, vanilla
ice cream, and fruit. The wines were sherry, madeira, claret,
"and probably others."

It is a wonder we have any stomachs at all, being descended
as we are from the men of the nineteenth century.

VII

Hawthorne had perhaps a half dozen intimate friends [writes
W. M. White]: the political threesome of Bridge, Cilley, and Pierce
from college days; Bright during the period in England; Ticknor
and Fields, his publishers, late in life. Among writers, Hawthorne
formed close but not overly intimate friendships with Thoreau,
Longfellow, and Melville. It is significant that the companionship
of practical men like Franklin Pierce and Horatio Bridge was preferred to that of the Emerson and Alcott variety.

The coolness between Emerson and Hawthorne was not
discreditable to either man; it was due to a lack of consan-
guinity of temperament and not to any coldness of heart on
either side. Hawthorne felt more hold on reality in Thoreau;
on the other hand, Thoreau was far more of a "come-outer"
than Emerson, with much less of social accommodation about
him. "You will find him well worth knowing," he wrote Longfellow; "he is a man of thought and originality, with a certain
iron-poker-ishness, an uncompromising stiffness in his mental
character, which is interesting, though it grows rather wearisome on close and frequent acquaintance." Concerning Longfellow himself Hawthorne seems to have had no reservations
but he showed no great eagerness to accept his invitations.

Of Melville Hawthorne saw a good deal at Lenox, after
Melville had written his now famous "Hawthorne and His
Mosses," one of the first adequate appreciations of Hawthorne's
genius. Hawthorne did not at first wish to meet his admirer,
but, having done so, he immediately invited him to come and

stay in his house. Their last meeting was many years later in England, where, as Hawthorne somewhat wearily observed, Melville persisted in "wandering to-and-fro" over the deserts of fruitless metaphysical speculation, "as dismal and monotonous as the sand hills amid which we were sitting. He can neither believe, nor be comfortable in his unbelief; and he is too honest and courageous not to try to do one or the other." Hawthorne could not respond in kind to Melville's rhapsodic transports; he had not the temperament for that; but it is silly to pretend that he failed Melville in his friendship. *Moby-Dick* was dedicated to him and according to Melville Hawthorne enlarged his own comprehension of its meaning.[17]

When one wearies of the eulogies of Hawthorne's admirers, it is always safe to turn to Woodberry for relief. "It is plain," says Woodberry, "that Pierce was the only man that Hawthorne loved with his full heart."

Pierce's devotion to Hawthorne needs no arguing. Not only did he care for him at the end; he looked after Julian in college; in September 1868, when Mrs. Hawthorne was planning to remove her family to Europe, she asked him to lend her $1000. ("Can you spare so much to the family of your dearest friend? I prefer to ask you rather than anyone else, because I think my husband would have preferred to be indebted to you than anyone.")

Hawthorne, too, passed the test when he refused his publisher's request not to dedicate *Our Old Home* to Pierce because of his intense unpopularity in the Civil War North:

My long and intimate personal relations with Pierce render the dedication altogether proper, especially as regards this book, which would have had no existence without his kindness; and if he is so exceedingly unpopular that his name is enough to sink this volume, there is so much the more need that an old friend should stand by him. I cannot, merely on account of pecuniary profit or literary reputation, go back from what I have deliberately felt and thought it right to do; and if I were to tear out the dedication, I should never look at the volume again without remorse and shame. As for the literary public, it must accept my book precisely as I see fit to give it, or let it alone.

Yet there are utterances of Hawthorne's concerning Pierce (and Cilley too) which are all the more startling in their cold-blooded honesty when we place them beside such an emotional passage as this.[18] Both men belonged to the genus politician, and Hawthorne had no illusions about that animal even when he chanced to have domesticated a specimen. The campaign biography was an act of kindness which long preceded *Our Old Home*, and Hawthorne knew that this too had cost him the regard of his friends. Pierce "certainly owes me something," he said. Much later, when he was trying to get the Honolulu consulship for Bridge, he wrote Mrs. Bridge that Pierce's friendship, though genuine, was more "practical" than "sentimental." Pierce would not have appointed Hawthorne to Liverpool if he had not believed him the best man for the post, and Bridge could not expect Honolulu unless he should be similarly convinced. "I never knew or heard of a man at once so warm and so cold, so subtile and so true, as Franklin Pierce." Later Hawthorne tried to get a minor appointment in England for Ticknor's son. Pierce could have no objection, he assured Ticknor, "but it would be just like him to let the whole matter slip, from pure negligence."

W. C. Brownell found Hawthorne lacking in initiative, and Woodberry complains again that "at every stage [he] was materially aided by his friends in obtaining employment and position." In his youth his sisters ran his errands; in later years his publishers did. It is really startling, in going through his letters to Ticknor and Fields, to see how much Hawthorne required of them. He wouldn't go to Washington unless

Ticknor went with him; he wouldn't go to Liverpool unless Ticknor took him to the boat. Ticknor even saw to it that Pierce did not forget to make the appointment. He bought clothes for Hawthorne—and a watch for his wife—and he went to Concord to look after Hawthorne's property during his absence. Hawthorne decided without consulting him to have 500 copies of Delia Bacon's book imprinted with the Ticknor and Fields imprint and sent them to Ticknor to be sold in America. Ticknor even sent him pens to write with. On the other hand, when Ticknor wanted some ale and cheese from England, it took Hawthorne four months to get around to sending them. Even after his death, his family continued this course. Rose in Concord sends Mrs. Fields shopping in Boston for a straw hat, and Una sends her braid and sewing silk to match. Una also asks Fields himself to get tickets for Booth and for Ristori.

As I have said elsewhere, I do not see how Hawthorne could have been expected to appoint himself to the customs or consular service, but there is no denying that he did have a gift for being served. Independent as his character was in all essential aspects, he seems to have had no objection to depending on his friends in practical and material matters.

CHAPTER FOUR

THE CITIZEN

I

In politics as such Hawthorne had little interest. It is true that when he was in England he was shocked by the political indifference of the people, but he had no right to be, for he once stated that he himself could not understand a newspaper until it was a hundred years old. In 1841 he professed hardly to remember the name of the President, and in 1849 he claimed to have voted only twice since he had been appointed to office. Whether or not this was literally true, many of the Salem Democrats hardly knew he belonged to them until he had been thrown out of office for being a Democrat.

Toward politicians as such he was always inclined to be superior. "Their hearts wither away, and die out of their bodies. Their consciences are turned to India-rubber—or to some substance as black as that, and which will stretch as much." Even political friends win only a qualified approval. "He has wasted much of his life in politics," he once wrote of John L. O'Sullivan, "but is a scholar, and might have been a poet, and is well known in our literature by his former editorship of the Democratic review, & above all, he is one of the truest and best men in the world." Hawthorne showed his political perspicacity when he outlined Franklin Pierce's career to him in advance upon his election to the New Hampshire House of Representatives. "Nothing can keep Frank Pierce from being President," he once told Fields. "Remember someday what I now tell you!" Yet for all Hawthorne's loyalty to Pierce, from the moment he became involved in politics he was a member of a class as well as an individual, and Hawthorne could not forget that for the class he had little respect. "I hardly know whether to congratulate you," he wrote when his friend was nominated, "for it would be absurd to suppose that the great office to which you are destined will ever afford you one happy or comfortable moment—and yet it is an end worthy of all ambition, as the highest *success* that this whole world offers to a statesman." Later, struggling with the campaign biography, he added, "I sometimes wish the convention had nominated old Cass! It would have saved you and me a great deal of trouble but my share of it will terminate four years sooner than your own."

Yet Hawthorne was not without political convictions. He was certainly not without political conditioning. He grew up in a town torn between the Federalists who opposed the War of 1812 and the Democrats who supported it, and the line of division cut through Hawthorne's own relationships, for his mother's family, the Mannings, were Federalists, while the Hawthornes, who had come down in the world since colonial times, were Jeffersonians or Democrats. Once during the war a cousin of Hawthorne's was jailed for leading Jeffersonians in a riot. Hawthorne's father had been a professed Democrat, and an uncle held public office on the Democratic ticket.[1]

The consciousness of lost family stature may have inclined Hawthorne toward the Democrats, but if so it was certainly reinforced by other influences and considerations. It was not only in "The Procession of Life" that he preferred to classify people by their spiritual condition rather than by the position they chanced to occupy upon the social ladder. Hawthorne was never a "radical" in any modern sense of the term, but in the abstract he was able to contemplate the possibility of a

classless society quite without terror. The Pyncheon aristoc-
racy is a handicap in the present state of the world's affairs,
and it does not occur to anybody to inquire whether or not
Phoebe (to whom the future clearly belongs, whatever may
be thought of her as a piece of characterization) is a "lady."
All his life Hawthorne wanted power in the hands of the local
government, the direct representatives of the people, and he
opposed the centralization of power and the assumption of any
activities on the part of the Federal government which make
for such centralization. Even in *The American Magazine* under
his editorship such Federalists as John Adams and Alexander
Hamilton were viewed with a distinctly critical eye.

Being what he was, it seems strange that Hawthorne should
have been, as Randall Stewart remarks, "involved in politics,
either as an office-seeker or an office holder, for twenty years."
He did not like it; in a sense it even gave him a feeling of
unreality to go through with it. But he did it, and he did it
well. He played the game, too, under the rules which had been
formulated for it. A beneficiary of the spoils system, he was
quite willing to have others removed to make room for him,
and while he was consul at Liverpool he even succeeded in
keeping the Manchester agency vacant for three years in order
that he might pocket the fees which would otherwise have
gone to his subordinate.

Hawthorne liked to take up the pose of having written
Pierce's life unwillingly, out of pure disinterested friendship
and with no thought of reward. But the evidence shows clearly
that he broached the idea to Pierce, though in a characteristically tentative and half-hearted fashion—"Mr. Hazewell, now,
I believe, the editor of the *Boston Times*," might, he thought,
do a better job—before Pierce had had a chance to suggest it
to him. It is clear, too, that from the beginning he knew that
there would be a political plum for him if Pierce were elected,

and he did not think it "wrong" to accept this, though there
was, no doubt, a certain species of condescension in his acceptance of it. After Pierce's election he was widely regarded as a
man of influence, and he does not seem to have been unwilling
to be consulted. His letters show considerable political tact,
wisdom, and caution. He mediated between opposing men and
forces and strove to prevent troublesome issues from coming
to a head. He tried to get offices for his friends (unsuccessfully
in Melville's case) and gave wise, worldly, sometimes slightly
cynical advice. He would not have been human if he had not
in a measure enjoyed this unwonted eminence, and Mrs. Longfellow was probably quite right when she judged him as looking "quite radiant for him" after his own appointment.

It is not too much to say that Hawthorne's first fame
followed his removal from his post at Salem, which made him
the subject of public controversy. But while he was quite
justified in the indignation he felt and expressed, he was far
from accurate in taking up the position that he had been given
his post as a man of letters rather than a deserving Democrat,
or that it had come to him without solicitation on his part.
It would be too severe, however, to call him mendacious in
the pose he assumed. He *was* innocent of the charges his
enemies made against him. He *had* performed his duties faith-
fully, and he was so far from having wronged his Whig sub-
ordinates that he had actually weakened his support among the
Democrats by not turning them all out. Moreover the *real*
Hawthorne really did feel the aloofness he professed, for the
real Hawthorne had never been in the custom house at all.
He had accepted political appointment for financial necessity
but he had never *meant* any of this! He was a star astray within
the bright moon's nether tip. Inner space is always more important than outer space to a man like Hawthorne, and it is
inner space that he must primarily keep on terms with. There

is an element of casuistry and self-deception here, but it was not greater in Hawthorne's case than it is with other men.

II

A special topic in connection with Hawthorne's attitude toward public affairs is his attitude toward England—and toward Europe in general. On first consideration this seems less that of an American patriot than a patrioteer. "After all the slander against Americans, there is no people worthy even to take the second place behind us, for liberality of idea and practice. The more I see of the rest of the world, the better I think of my own country." In England everything is wrong from government to trees to women. The English eat twice as much as the Americans (but their food is miserable); their climate is miserable too; and they themselves are dirty and ugly and greedy and coarse. When you do find an attractive Englishman, you find, as in Leigh Hunt's case, that his mother was an American! Once, when he was pleased with a party, Hawthorne even resolved the paradox on the ground that most of its members were Irish!

Not that the Irish—or anybody else—got a clean bill of health. Historic places stank all over Europe. The Scots, though better looking than the English, were also more drunken. Paris was magnificent materially but its French inhabitants ruined it. As for Rome, well, what can you do with a people who relieve themselves in the Forum? "I bitterly detest Rome, and shall rejoice to bid it farewell forever, and I dully acquiesce in all the mischief and ruin that has happened to it, from Nero's conflagration downward. In fact, I wish the very site had been obliterated before I ever saw it." Even London, fog and all, looked better after he had been in Rome. All things considered, however, it was the Germans who received the warmest compliment: the Germans were "the meanest devils in the world."

Perhaps Hawthorne expected more of the English than he did of the others; at the same time he was certainly more prejudiced against them. It seems doubtful that he ever really looked at the English people. He saw them through a mist of prejudices left over from two wars whose distorting effect, not only upon his eyesight but upon that of generations of Americans, we now find it difficult to estimate or to understand. The stereotype "Englishman" which he carried in his mind possessed him to such an extent that it blotted out the real Englishmen he met, none of whom, he admitted, exemplified it. There was an "acrid" quality about the English that he could not endure; their arrogance repelled him; they thought so well of themselves that there was really no necessity for anybody else to think about them at all. "It is only as an American that I am hostile to England, and because she hates us. Individually, I like almost every Englishman I know, and they certainly are very kind to me. . . . So you can judge of the strength of my public virtue, that it counterbalances so much private feeling!"

There had always been a conflict in Hawthorne between the conservative and the iconoclast. All his work testifies that he felt the appeal of old things, old beauties. At the same time he felt the burden of the past as an accumulation of rubbish. Holgrave's famous diatribes in *The House of the Seven Gables* are dramatic utterances [2]—and Holgrave himself is won away from them in the course of the narrative. But Hawthorne goes almost as far *in propria persona*—in fiction in *The Marble Faun*, where he writes that all towns should be burned down every fifty years, and in life, where he was so oppressed by the accumulations in the British Museum that he wished both the Elgin Marbles and the frieze of the Parthenon reduced to lime! Overattachment to the past is dramatized in Lady Eleanore, Hepzibah Pyncheon, Peter Goldthwaite, and "The White Old

Maid"; and Harry Levin may well be right in suggesting that
the moral of "My Kinsman, Major Molineux" is that Robin
must now forget the past and stand on his own feet in the
living present.[3] Literary accumulations go into the bonfire of
"Earth's Holocaust" along with other things; even in nature
Hawthorne felt that this year's growth was hindered by last
year's dead leaves. In the last unfinished works—"let the past
alone"—the domination of things gone by has become almost an
obsession.

England—or Europe—was the past to Hawthorne; at her
best an accumulation of *objets d'art*, at her worst a political
anachronism, using her blood-encrusted, monarchical, caste-
ridden power to delay the triumph of the democratic and
Democratic, American and "Young America" principles to
which Hawthorne adhered. And though he saw England as
definitely on the downgrade—America would never need her
in the future, but she would find herself in desperate need of
America—yet the old serpent still had enough sting left in her
tail to be well worthy of hatred. Once he suggested that by
1900 England would be a minor republic under the protection
of the United States. Sometimes, not too seriously, he pon-
dered the idea of America's annexing Britain. It might even
be good for us to live with "more simple and natural people"
than ourselves. But if any adaptation between the powers was
to be called for, he was all in favor of having Britain make it.
Sometimes he suggests Colonel McCormick's reply to the
people who, in the 1940's, were advocating "Union with
Britain Now." If Britain really wanted union with the United
States, inquired the Chicago *Tribune*, what was to prevent her
from applying for admission as a state to the Federal Union?

But Hawthorne was not consistent. During his last years in
Europe he made every conceivable statement about wanting
to leave and wanting to stay. He was homesick, but he did not

wish to return to America under the conditions which now prevailed there. He loved Concord and the Old Corner Bookstore, but the rest of the country could go hang as far as he was concerned. He feared he had lost his country by staying away too long. He knew the United States was good for many purposes, but he questioned whether it was fit to live in; if it were not for the children he might never come home at all. And much, much more to the same effect and to every conceivable opposed effect. Even after he had returned, there were times when he wished he were in Europe again, and after he was dead Mrs. Hawthorne told Mrs. Fields he disliked Concord so much that when he departed with Pierce upon his last journey, she had vowed that he should never need to come back there; she would find him a place "by his beloved sea." She liked to think of him, she said, in England and at Monte Beni, "where he enjoyed himself as nowhere else, as far as surroundings went."

Partly this is the familiar Hawthorne restlessness, and partly it is his lack of harmonious adjustment to Civil War America. But partly it is also the fact that, for all his criticisms and complaints, he had responded to a great deal of what he had seen abroad; from the time of his foreign residence on he was a man with a divided heart. In one 1855 letter he speaks of himself as being more at home in London than in Boston or Salem. "Being the great metropolis of the world, it is every man's home." And not only London but even Rome; for all the bitter things he had said about it, and for all the anguish he had suffered there during Una's illness, it had cast its spell, and he wanted to see it again.

He looked for his own name on English gravestones; in a sense he was looking for his own roots. And why should we be surprised by this since, as Harry Levin reminds us, not only the Anglophile Henry James reflected this same feeling (*The*

Sense of the Past) but even the aggressively American Mark Twain (*The American Claimant*). Hawthorne sounded like Mark Twain when he told Howells that he "wished he could find some part of America 'where the cursed shadow of Europe had not fallen.' " But surely he was not searching for roots but tearing them up when he foolishly declared that he wished America might herself become a monarchy. Here is an inconsistency that neither Emerson nor Whitman nor Mark Twain himself ever surpassed. Small American homes never looked as good to Hawthorne again after he had been in England; he now wanted to live in a manor house; and the best argument he could think of for annexing England was that he could then end all his conflicts and have an estate in Warwickshire. When he arrived in France he was surprised how English he had grown in five years. "If England were all the world," he once cried in a moment of enthusiasm, "it would still have been worth while for the Creator to have made it."

III

In the great characteristic reform movement of nineteenth-century America—abolition—Hawthorne took no part, a circumstance which estranged him in later years from both his sisters-in-law and from most of his peers among writers, who, to his way of thinking, viewed the slavery question "with an awful squint." He misrepresents himself when he writes in a letter, "I have not . . . the slightest sympathy for the slaves," though he is no doubt accurate when he continues, "or at least, not half so much as for the laboring whites, who, I believe, as a general thing, are ten times worse off than the Southern negroes." Slavery was an evil nevertheless—the Fugitive Slave Law roused the same kind of indignation in him as it did in other New Englanders—and he expected it to disappear in the course of time. He differed from his abolitionist contemporaries in his steadfast refusal to pluck the slavery evil out of its context, his determination to view it as part of the warp and woof of a fallen world. To fail in this was to achieve a monstrously warped and unbalanced view of life, and to try to tear this one evil up by the roots, regardless of what other plants were uprooted with it, was to run the risk of destroying the whole garden. It was because Franklin Pierce steadfastly rejected this approach that Hawthorne persisted in regarding him as a wise man.

Hawthorne's heart sympathized with the reformers even when his head told him that they were wrong. He did not even reject as such the characteristically nineteenth-century faith in "progress." Specifically he thought it better for a young man never to have been born than not to believe, and for a mature man to die rather than relinquish the faith, "that we are not doomed to creep on forever in the old bad way." He himself spoke out against dueling. He was at least seriously skeptical of the wisdom and the necessity of capital punishment. "The best of us being unfit to die, what an inexpressible absurdity to put the worst to death!" And when, as consul at Liverpool, he learned what a floating hell the merchant service had become, he undertook vainly a one-man crusade to get laws passed which would correct these evils. His son-in-law George Lathrop afterwards stated that he even planned to continue his agitation by writing a book or a series of articles after his return to America, a scheme which the Civil War prevented him from carrying out. We know that he blamed Charles Sumner greatly for his failure to engage in this crusade, ascribing his indifference to absorption in the slavery issue, and rather amusingly failing to perceive that maggot for maggot he and Sumner were quite in the same boat.[4]

In general, however, Hawthorne recognized the need of reform and at the same time gravely doubted its efficacy. About the effect of reform on the character of the reformer, however, he was considerably more than doubtful. In his eyes reformers in general were egotists, malcontents, and misfits —"crooked sticks"—who found a more effective outlet for their intolerance and passion for domination in reform activities than other people find in frankly selfish domination and self-indulgence. They who love causes, not men, are always prepared to sacrifice a man to a cause, and in general suffer themselves to be warped out of a normal, symmetrical course of development by a ruling passion. Even the fact that the passion is benevolent—or was at the outset—does not make it impossible that it should at last turn the man who cherishes it into a monster.[5] Even at Brook Farm he noticed that the effect of reform activity was to estrange those who adopted it from the society they wished to serve and to save. He embodied all these faults in the character of Hollingsworth in the novel he wrote about his Brook Farm experiences, and Moncure D. Conway was so impressed by the portrait that he decided on the spot that he would not be that kind of reformer.

Hawthorne could not believe that even a great man might achieve a reform except as an agent of the spirit of the age that was ready to effect that reform.[6] He did not favor the interference of government in the common welfare until it had clearly been shown to be indispensable. Nor did he think any man really wise enough to be a reformer. Those who tried to do good often achieved evil, as his own ancestors had done when they persecuted witches and Quakers, and even when a real evil was destroyed it might give birth, in dying, to another more monstrous than itself. "The good of others, like our own happiness, is not to be attained by direct effort, but inciden-

tally. . . . I am really too humble to think of doing good!"
When they visited the Manassas battlefield, Hawthorne and
Edward Dicey met some runaway slaves. They gave them
food and money and put them on a northbound train. But
Hawthorne's conscience was as hard to satisfy as Huckleberry
Finn's; it plagued him no matter what he did. "I am not sure
that we were doing right after all," he told Dicey afterwards.
"How can these poor beings find food and shelter away from
home?" It was the same with the consulate, where he had
exerted himself for many people and at least one cause. "I only
know that I have done no good—none whatever." And he
dogmatizes: "There is no instance, in all history, of the human
will and intellect having perfected any great moral reform
by methods which it adopted to that end."

Where does this leave us, then? Do we sit back comfortably
and do nothing, confident that God will solve all our problems
for us in His own good time? In a measure Hawthorne does
leave himself open to the charge of having advocated this.
So he tells us of Holgrave in *The House of the Seven Gables*
that he was not wrong in his faith that there was a good time
coming.

His error lay in supposing that this age, more than any past or
future one, is destined to see the tattered garments of Antiquity
exchanged for a new suit, instead of gradually renewing themselves
by patchwork; in applying his own little life-span as the measure of
an interminable achievement; and, more than all, in fancying that
it mattered anything to the great end in view whether he himself
should contend for it or against it.

But it is certainly Hawthorne's due that we should recognize
and make allowance for the really respectable theological
background which his point of view, even when it has been
stated at its worst, can command, for basically all anti-Pelagians
must stand with him. Hawthorne really did believe in Provi-

dence, and because he knew that God is wiser than men, he never made the mistake of imagining that men must do God's work for Him while leaving their own undone. This often helped him to achieve a balance which we find it difficult or impossible to secure. It made his Aylmer in "The Birthmark" a prototype of all scientists and all learned fools who, unable to accept the inevitable limitations of human life, mar and destroy God's work in seeking to improve it; it also gave him the wisdom to perceive, as he proclaimed in "Earth's Holocaust," that there is no use casting human follies and vanities into the bonfire unless you are prepared to cast the human heart, which is their source, in after them.

But Hawthorne does not really leave us with a choice only between a direct attack upon evil and a craven surrender to it. He knew, as medieval men knew, that sometimes a flank attack is more effective, and that some evils are best dealt with by ignoring them.

Men who have spent their lives in generous and holy contemplation for the human race; those who, by a certain heavenliness of spirit, have purified the atmosphere around them, and thus supplied a medium in which good and high things may be projected and performed—give to these a lofty place among the benefactors of mankind, although no deed, such as the world calls deeds, may be recorded of them.

This is the way all true contemplatives function, but—what is more to the point—it is also the way all worthy artists function *when they are functioning as artists*. This is obviously a very slow way of attacking evil, and there is always a grave danger that the world may be blown up in the meantime. But in the long run it builds the kind of atmosphere in which the gains won by more impulsive reformers can alone be expected to survive, and which may at last even make their strenuous activities unnecessary.

IV

Because Hawthorne was the only great New England writer except the Quaker Whittier who did not wholeheartedly support the Civil War, modern pacifists are sometimes tempted to make a hero of him, while on the other hand, the patrioteers excoriate him as having been corrupted by his association with Franklin Pierce. Neither view is defensible. Hawthorne did not agree with Franklin Pierce, whose views on the war were far more consistent and reasonable. Hawthorne had brilliant flashes of insight, as when he perceived that at best the war would "only effect by a horrible convulsion the self-same end that might and would have been brought about by gradual and peaceful change," and we can afford to forgive him much for the rough, salutary, Johnsonian common sense revealed in his reply to Emerson's statement that John Brown made the gallows as venerable as the cross; Hawthorne said that no man ever deserved hanging more.[7] Taken as a whole, however, Hawthorne's Civil War utterances are not impressive from either a pacifist or an anti-pacifist point of view. He gives no sign of having understood the real issues involved. At his worst he was merely frivolous.

It is true, of course, that military glory had never appealed to Hawthorne. In college he was indifferent to drill, and his contributions to *The American Magazine* had a distinctly anti-war tinge. He regretted "that men of the sword . . . should hitherto have filled so large a space in the annals of every nation" and that "the Greek Church and the Roman Church should shed blood for the privilege of celebrating Mass in the Holy Sepulchre." Even the "poetry" in the juvenile "Spectator" takes a rather anti-war tone.

He loathed war memorials. "I heartily wish that every trophy of victory might crumble away," he said. Even the

Concord battlefield beside his home at the Old Manse, which people came from far and wide to see, left him cold. "For my own part, I have never found my imagination much excited by this or any other scene of historical celebrity; nor would the placid margin of the river have lost any of its charm for me had men never fought and died there." In his eyes a professional soldier was a professional ruffian. The only men fit to be professional soldiers were those fit for nothing else, and when nature gave a man no gifts "she must be understood as intending him for a soldier." Even the portraits of illustrious warriors generally looked stupid. War robs women of husbands and lovers and ruins even those it spares and sends home again; every army camp demoralizes the countryside around it, the women as well as the men.

Hawthorne took special care to tear down military glory in his writings for children. His attitude appears in "The Dragon's Teeth" and in "The Great Stone Face"; it also appears in *Grandfather's Chair*. Grandfather has no time to talk about battles, and he thinks John Eliot preaching to the Indians a grander figure than General Wolfe on the Plains of Abraham.

Of course this does not mean that Hawthorne's writings about American history are devoid of patriotism. In general he lauds and glorifies the principles for which the rebellious colonists contended; in general he condemns the "aristocrats" who opposed them. He was also much given to praise of Andrew Jackson, who, as one of the first great Democrats, was distinctly one of his weaknesses. But in general his patriotism was a sectional patriotism, as the Civil War showed. Although he recognized the dangers of inbreeding, it seemed to him that in a large, federated nation, patriotism must take on a specialized character; his heart was simply not large enough to embrace the whole country; he could not love what he did not know. Once he even declared that he "hated" naturalized

citizens: "Nobody has a right to our ideas unless born to them."
As he envisaged it, the Federal government was more ruthless
than paternal, and the eagle was a good symbol for it. Basically
he was content to have it so, for he knew that when an American "leans on the mighty arm of the Republic, his own proper
strength departs from him."

He refused to be seduced by Italian patriotism while he was
in Italy; during the Crimean War he sympathized with Russia,
not England. And when British-American relations were
strained during the 'fifties, he acted like a little boy kicking
up dust on the playground. "I begin to feel warlike, too. There
was a rumor yesterday, that our minister had demanded his
passports; and I am mistaken in Frank Pierce if Mr. Crampton
has not already been ejected from Washington." Hawthorne
would not say that he wanted war, but he was not willing to
"bate an inch of honor" to avoid it; he wanted England to be
humiliated, and he had an idea that if we did not fight her now
we could never fight her at all. When Fields so far failed to
share his views as to declare that if war came he would fight
for England, Hawthorne was outraged: "I hope he will live
to be tarred and feathered, and that I may live to pour the first
ladleful of tar on the top of his head, and to clap the first
handful of feathers on the same spot. He is a traitor, and his
English friends know it; for they speak of him as one of themselves." When the crisis was past, he hailed the triumph of
Pierce diplomacy, teaching England new respect for the United
States.

To be sure these were all private utterances, and some of
them may be set down to blowing off steam. When Hawthorne was called upon to make a public address in England
during the crisis, he was gracious and conciliatory, even offering a toast to the British army as a means of indicating he
believed war to be out of the question. But twisting the British

lion's tail was a sport to which Hawthorne was predisposed by more than his convictions about the Revolution or his memories of the War of 1812. Through his association with John L. O'Sullivan, George N. Sanders, and others, he was, in some measure, involved in the notorious "Young America" movement, which was supported by German and Italian immigrants and by Tammany Hall. "Young America" favored a vigorous foreign policy and the military and naval forces to back it up; it even inclined to advocate American intervention in behalf of democratic movements abroad. Hawthorne's connection with it cannot be entirely explained in terms of its support of Pierce or even its stand for social equality. "I should like to know what is to become of us at sea, in case of war," he once wrote Charles Sumner—"but *that* you don't care about." As American consul at London, Sanders placed diplomatic despatch bags at the service of European revolutionists, made his own living quarters a center for revolutionary conspiracies, and finally himself advocated the assassination of Louis Napoleon. The Senate refused to confirm his appointment, and he was recalled to America in 1854. Hawthorne's consequent expression of "regret and mortification" and his hope that Pierce would do "the right and honorable thing" are hard to reconcile with the good judgment he manifested elsewhere. How could the same man who believed John Brown deserved hanging defend such a fool as Sanders? How could he be so aware as he was of the abolitionist danger to peace in the United States and support such a dangerous policy abroad?

We get one vivid glimpse of how Hawthorne conducted himself among his Concord neighbors during the Civil War in Rebecca Harding Davis's description of Bronson Alcott holding forth patriotically in the parlor at The Wayside:

Mr. Emerson stood listening, his head sunk on his breast, with profound submissive attention, but Hawthorne sat astride a chair, his arms folded on his back, his chin dropped on them, and his laughing, sagacious eyes watching us, full of mockery. . . . Mr. Hawthorne at last gathered himself up lazily to his feet, and said quietly: "We cannot see that thing at so long a range. Let us go to dinner," and Mr. Alcott suddenly checked the droning flow of his prophecy and quickly led the way to the dining-room.

In letters to his friends he was less reserved. He approved of the war, but he did not

quite understand what we are fighting for, or what definite result can be expected. If we pummel the South ever so hard, they will love us none the better for it; and even if we subjugate them, our next step should be to cut them adrift. . . . Whatever happens next, I must say that I rejoice that the old Union is smashed. . . . People must die, whether a bullet kills them or no; and money must be spent, if not for gunpowder, then for worse luxuries. My country-men choose to spend themselves and their property in war; and they find, at this very moment, an enjoyment in it worth all their sacrifices.

The Union defeat at Bull Run got under his skin, and there were times when he even wished he were young enough to volunteer himself. On the other hand, he thought it unreason-able to wish his countrymen to kill each other "for the sake of refreshing my palled spirits," and so he decided to "pray for peace."

The *Monitor* frightened him as a portent of future mecha-nized warfare, and he feared that if the war were successful, it would militarize America for years to come. When he went with Julian to stay at Prides Crossing, he wrote Rose that he had seen no papers and had no idea "whether the rebels have taken Washington"; and when he himself came back to Wash-ington with Ticknor from Fortress Monroe in 1862, while the Vice-President and the rest of the party went farther south, he speculated impishly on whether the "rebels" might not have caught "every mother's son of them—and daughters too, for there were a good many ladies among them. That would be an excellent joke; and nothing would please me better, if Mr. and Mrs. Bridge were not among them." In a letter to his English friend Francis Bennoch he proposed that nobody under fifty should be taken into the army, with "a premium in favor of recruits of three-score years and upwards."

On July 4, 1863, Hawthorne went to Concord, New Hampshire, with Franklin Pierce and sat on the platform while Pierce attacked Lincoln and the war. Hawthorne's own candid camera shot of Lincoln in the essay "Chiefly of War Matters" is not slanderous, but he more than once declared that he "despised" the administration "with all my heart." This, however, was about the only important point with reference to the war on which Hawthorne and Pierce were agreed. Pierce never wavered in his adherence to "the grand idea of an irrevocable Union." He opposed the war because he did not believe "aggression by arms" was "a suitable or possible remedy for existing evils." Throughout the war he stood publicly for an immediate armistice and a return to the *status quo ante bellum*.

To Hawthorne this was sentimental. "It would be too great an absurdity to spend all our Northern strength for the next generation in holding on to a people who insist on being let loose." For himself he had "never loved" the South anyway. "We do not belong together, the Union is unnatural, a scheme of man, not an ordinance of God." After it had broken up, New England would "still have her rocks and ice, and a nobler people than ever heretofore."

Hawthorne would fight, therefore, neither to free the slaves nor to preserve the Union. But why, then, fight at all? Why not, as Horace Greeley once expressed it, let our erring sisters go? Because

if we had not fought, the North would unquestionably have lost its Capital, and its identity as a nation, and would have had to make

an entirely new position for itself, and possibly three or four separate positions. If we stop fighting at this juncture [November 14,
1861], we give up Maryland, Virginia, Kentucky, Missouri, all of
which are fully capable of being made free soil, and will be so in
a few years if we possess them, but not in a hundred years if we
lose them.

In a letter to Elizabeth Peabody written in the summer of
1863, Hawthorne went so far as to hope that recent Northern
victories might cause Confederates to see

that their best hope lies in the honor of the peace Democrats of
the North . . . by amalgamation with whom I really think that the
old Union might be restored and slavery prolonged for another
hundred years with new bulwarks; while the people of the North
would fancy that they had got their victory and never know that
they shed their blood in vain, and so would become peace Democrats to a man.

But he did not actually think that feasible. What he did
believe was that the best solution was "a separation of the
Union giving us the west bank of the Mississippi and a boun-
dary line affording as much Southern soil as we can hope to
digest into freedom in another century." Inasmuch, then, as
Hawthorne was consistent at all in his Civil War attitudes,
he advocated prosecuting the war so that the North might be
in a position to dictate peace terms and establish the best
conditions possible for the continued existence of a northern
and western free state.

CHAPTER FIVE

THE FIRE IN THE MEMBERS

I

Nothing has been said so far concerning Hawthorne's relationship to the most basic of human passions. We must not allow his high moral principles and undeviating rectitude of conduct to obscure the fact that he was a passionate man, "having an appetite for the brown bread and the tripe and sausages of life." It is as certain as anything of this kind can be that he came to his wife as virginal as she came to him, but this was not for want of susceptibility or the power to be tempted. One of his complaints about Englishmen was that they lacked proper respect for girls of the lower classes. And though he seems to have had little to do with girls during his college years, it is still abundantly clear that he knew how to look at them.

At Thomaston, Maine, in 1837 there was the "frank, free, mirthful daughter of the landlady, about twenty-four years old, between whom and myself there immediately sprang up a flirtation which made us both feel rather solemn when we parted on Tuesday morning." Fortunately this did not prevent him from responding to "music in the evening, with a song by a rather pretty, fantastic little mischief of a brunette, about eighteen years old," whose "manner of walking" was "by jerks, with a quiver, as if she were made of calves-feet jelly." When he was at North Adams the next year he is said to have presented the tavern-keeper's niece with a copy of *Twice-Told Tales;* it is interesting that the same person who remembered this described him as walking along the street "with his eyes down." [1] Then there was the lovely girl at Swampscott whose attraction for him he fictionalized in "The Village Uncle," who was "sadly perplexed with the rude behavior of the wind" about her petticoats, and who, "obeying nature, . . . did free things without indelicacy, displayed a maiden's thoughts to every age, and proved . . . [herself] as innocent as naked Eve." There may have been an abortive engagement to a girl named Eliza Gibbs, who lived on Martha's Vineyard,[2] and we do not know his exact relations with the mischief-making Mary Silsbee, later Mrs. Jared Sparks, whose malicious lies nearly got him involved in a duel with John O'Sullivan.[3] But we do know that he was already engaged to Sophia when he encountered at Brook Farm the little seamstress whom he wrote into *The Blithedale Romance*, and this did not inhibit an observation that was as keen and loving as it was clear-headed.

Hawthorne recognized his tendency to idealize women and girls. "I know these girls to be realities of flesh and blood, yet . . . they mingle like kindred creatures with the ideal beings of my mind." But he was never in any danger of forgetting the flesh and blood, and since he was a completely normal man, he was not repelled by it; neither did it lessen the woman's appeal to him or his respect for her. "One pretty damsel, with a beautiful pair of naked white arms, addressed a mirthful remark" to him on the journey chronicled in "The Canal-Boat," and it is clear that he found it stimulating to sleep

close to the crimson curtain,—the sexual division of the boat,— behind which I continually heard whispers and stealthy footsteps; the noise of a comb laid on the table or a slipper dropped on the floor; the twang, like a broken harpspring, caused by loosening a

tight belt; the rustling of a gown in its descent; and the unlacing of
a pair of stays. My ears seemed to have the properties of an eye
—a visible image pestered my fancy in the darkness; the curtain was
withdrawn between me and the western lady, who yet disrobed herself without a blush.

He thought a white stocking "infinitely more effective than
a black one," and when little girls went wading he wanted
them to show "bare little legs," not pantalettes. "Her breasts
swell out round and soft," he writes of a countrywoman in
1837, "being abundant with milk for a little she-brat of three
or four months old—her first child, though she is not a very
young woman." As late as 1850 we find him meditating over
the life going on in some houses he observes from a distance,
ending with the upper chambers, where he observes, "here and
there, a light where perchance some lovely damsel is disrobing
herself for bed."

The American Notebooks have, too, a fascinating and
detailed description of two lower-class young women, with the
baby of one of them, whom Hawthorne watched at a popular
theater where a pantomime of *Jack the Giant Killer* was being
performed. Interest is here, and close observation, but—most
significantly—intense sympathy and a chivalrous determination
to have the best possible opinion of these girls, in spite of their
evident coarseness.

Hereupon, the smaller of the two girls, after a little inefficacious
dandling, at once settled the question of maternity, by uncovering
her bosom, and presenting it to the child, with so little care of
concealment that I saw, and anybody might have seen, the whole
breast, and the apex which the infant's little lips compressed. Yet
there was nothing indecent in this; but a perfect naturalness. . . .
I should like well to know who they are—and of what condition in
life—and whether reputable as members of the class to which they
belong. My own judgment is that they are so.

In London his sympathies ranged even farther beyond the bounds of prudery:

The streets were much thronged; and there seemed to be a good many young people—lovers, it is to be hoped—who had spent the day together, and were going innocently home. Perhaps so—perhaps not. At every street corner, too, under archways, and at other places of vantage, or loitering along, with some indescribable peculiarity that distinguished her, and perhaps turning to retread her footsteps, was a woman; or sometimes two walked arm in arm —hunting in couples—and separated when they saw a gentleman approaching. One feels a curious and reprehensible sympathy for these poor nymphs; it seems such a pity that they should not each and all of them find what they seek!—that any of them should tramp the pavement the whole night through, or should go hungry and forlorn to their beds.

II

Hawthorne is frequently berated for his objection to nudity in painting and sculpture. He entered no such objection in general terms. It is true that he sometimes objects to individual works. Titian was a frequent offender in his eyes; Raphael fell under the ban with *Fornarina;* and Rubens's "fair graces" might rather have been called "greases." He was ashamed to look at Gibson's colored statues, feeling that the coloring destroyed the chastity of the marble (though he admitted "something fascinating and delectable" about it too), and even Michelangelo's statues were judged to "sprawl, and fling their limbs abroad with adventurous freedom." But though it is disappointing to find Hawthorne rejecting so chaste a work as the *Greek Slave* of Hiram Powers—"it seems to me time to leave off sculpturing men and women naked; they mean nothing, and might as well bear one name as another, and belong to the same category as the ideal portraits in Books of Beauty, or in the windows of print-shops"—our disappointment does not excuse us from failing to note the true character of the objection. Hawthorne did not believe that sculpture could be a vital art unless the sculptor concerned himself with contemporary life, and it seemed to him ridiculous to carve a nude statue of a man whom nobody ever saw or thought of as nude.

Did anybody ever see Washington naked? It is inconceivable. He had no nakedness, but I imagine he was born with his clothes on, with his hair powdered, and made a stately bow on his first appearance in the world. His costume, at all events, was a part of his character, and must be dealt with by whatever sculptor undertakes to represent him.

But if nudity did not suit the subject—nor any modern subject—Hawthorne was quite clear that buttons and breeches were quite unsuited to the medium. Perhaps the logical solution would have been to devise some kind of conventional costume such as Sir Francis Legatt Chantry used for his arrangement of Washington's cloak in the statue at the Boston State House, but this too presented difficulties, and sometimes Hawthorne was tempted to pronounce the difficulties insuperable and set sculpture down as a lost art. However, he did not condemn naked statues he disliked any more severely than he condemned the purely conventional treatment of religious themes, for example, where no question of sexuality could intrude, or the use of allegory.

Of Hawthorne's admiration for the human body there can be no question. Charles Mackay has recorded that he once

expatiated at a length unusual for a man so taciturn, upon the perfect and incomparable beauty of the human form, asserting that it was utterly impossible for the wit or ingenuity of the wisest or most imaginative of men to suggest the slightest improvement upon its structure, its uses, and its loveliness, adding that the wings given by sculptors and painters to angels, were vulgar and monstrous distortions, making the angel a hybrid—half man, half bird.

He accepted Hiram Powers's *California* because it was not just a naked woman capable of exciting passion but an idealized figure; and in *The House of the Seven Gables* there is "a marble woman, to whom her own beauty was the sole and sufficient garment." The statues of Castor and Pollux in Rome he found "noble and godlike." But chastity did not mean sexlessness to Hawthorne; on the contrary he thought the chastity of a sexless figure meaningless and therefore repelllent. He was not shocked by the flaming sexuality of Veronese's *Rape of Europa*:

It must have been, in its day, the most brilliant and rejoicing picture, the most voluptuous, the most exuberant, that ever put the sunshine to shame. The bull has all Jupiter in him, so tender and gentle, yet so passionate, that you feel it indecorous to look at him; and Europa, under her thick, rich stuffs and embroideries, is all a woman. What a pity that such a picture should fade, and perplex the beholder with such splendor, shining through such forlornness!

It is in connection with Hawthorne's ardent, one-sided, yet finally fickle love affair with the *Venus de Medici*, however, that we may best observe his response to nude beauty in art. He first saw her on June 8, 1858, going through the gallery in mingled hope and fear of encountering her, lest she should disappoint him and extinguish "another of those lights that shine along a man's pathway." When he encountered her at last, somewhat unexpectedly, he immediately

felt a kind of tenderness for her; an affection, not as if she was one woman, but all womankind in one. Her modest attitude, which, before I saw her, I had not liked, deeming that it might be an artificial shame, is partly what unmakes her as a heathen goddess, and softens her into a woman. There is a slight degree of alarm, too, in her face; not that she really thinks anybody is looking at her, yet the idea has flitted through her mind, and startled her a little. Her face is so beautiful and intellectual, that it is not dazzled out of sight by her body.

It comforted him to think of her as deathless, "incapable of decay and death; as young and fair today as she was three thousand years ago, and still to be young and fair as long as a beautiful thought shall require physical embodiment." One might look at her "with new delight from infancy to old age, and keep the memory of her . . . as one of the treasures of spiritual existence hereafter."

A week later, Powers having attacked her on aesthetic grounds, he went to see her again, candidly and conscientiously studying the lovely face to see if he could find any foundation for the sculptor's strictures. He understood at last what Powers had meant, but he did not think it necessary to accept his conclusions. "Whatever rules may be transgressed, it is a noble and beautiful face,—more so, perhaps, than if all rules had been obeyed." But, alas for man's constancy! when he saw her again in September she seemed "little more than any other piece of yellowish white marble." On September 26 he threw his final glance at her "with strange insensibility."

Hawthorne does not appear to have been unduly fussy about nakedness in life or in the home either. Only a glance at Arthur Rackham's beautiful illustrations for "The Paradise of Children" in his edition of *A Wonder Book* is needed to remind us that Pandora and her comrades are gloriously naked throughout the story. Rackham is the only illustrator who, to my knowledge, has illustrated the text correctly from this point of view.

In the Red House at Lenox the bathroom was appropriately adorned with two pictures of Psyche "about to bathe and about to be dressed," and among the ornaments of Una's chambers at the Villa Montauto was "the representation of an undraped boy in wax, very prettily modeled, and holding up a heart that looks like a bit of red sealing wax." When, near Cambridge University, Hawthorne saw "troops of naked boys" bathing in the river in full view of all the world, it did not seem shameful to him; it was "Arcadia, in the simplicity of the Golden Age." Una and Julian were bathed together when they were small, and there is a charming pen picture of Una preparing for bed, and running about the room in her chemise, which does not come down far enough to serve the purpose of fig-leaf. Never were seen such contortions and attitudinizing— prostrating herself on all-fours, and thrusting up her little bum as a spectacle to men and angels, being among the least grotesque.

And Louisa May Alcott describes Rose at The Wayside, after the Hawthornes had returned from Europe, as "a little bud of a child with scarlet hair and no particular raiment, which is cool and artistic but somewhat startling to the common herd."

On the other hand, the Hawthorne children seem to have been taught little or nothing about sex, being told that they had been sent down from heaven, so that Julian at ten was still "glad he had happened to tumble into so good a family," and the girls at least would seem to most of us today to have been over-protected. Mrs. Hawthorne even rebuked her sister Elizabeth for writing about the evils of slavery in letters which Una might encounter. "She *never* reads newspapers." Waltzing was dangerous too—"fortunately Una shrinks from it"—and the Hawthornes would not send the girls to Sanborn's school in Concord because they disapproved of "this commingling of youths and maidens at the electric age." According to Sophia, Hawthorne fully shared her own horror of "this *flaring open* of girlhood and boyhood." And surely she takes high rank among the unconscious humorists in her agonized approach to the ghastly problem of Una's gymnasium dress after her father's death. It was not enough that her tunic and bloomers should come down below the knee as the other girls' did. They must come down to the tops of her shoes. "You shall wear your trousers and tunic, dear, and I shall not be distressed—if you cover up your legs entirely." And even though she was thus covered, she must not cross the street from her room to the school without wearing a skirt over her bloomers. But let us not, in the absence of evidence, assume that Hawthorne himself would have been guilty of this.

III

Hawthorne has surprisingly few comments on the moral tendencies of the books he read. He knew his Rabelais; once he expressed affection for the *Decameron*. In his review of Melville's *Typee* he found the descriptions of the native girls "voluptuously colored, yet not more so than the exigencies of the subject appear to require."

He has that freedom of view [Hawthorne continued]—it would be too harsh to call it laxity of principle—which renders him tolerant of codes of morals that may be little in accordance with our own; a spirit proper enough to a young and adventurous sailor, and which makes his book the more wholesome to our staid landsmen.

As for his own books, Hester of *The Scarlet Letter*, Zenobia of *The Blithedale Romance*, and Miriam of *The Marble Faun* are all voluptuous, slightly exotic women, but the only heroine of a short story who can be enrolled as a cadet in their company is the lovely and deeply moving Beatrice of "Rappaccini's Daughter," who "looked redundant with life, health, and energy; all of which attributes were bound down and compressed, as it were, and girdled tensely, in their luxuriance, by her virgin zone." Beatrice, to be sure, is one of the purest of girls. Hawthorne allowed her father to corrupt and pervert her physical nature, but (though he suggested something of the kind in Esther of "Ethan Brand") he did not allow him to destroy her soul, as Mrs. Black's soul is destroyed in that horrifying story, Arthur Machen's "The Inmost Light." Miriam may be pure also in the technical sense, but Hawthorne does not give us the material we should need to be quite sure. A number of critics have thought that the point of all the references to Beatrice Cenci is that Miriam too had been guilty of incest; [4] even if this is not the case, Hawthorne certainly brings the idea of incest into the story. Hester's adultery is of course the very mainspring of *The Scarlet Letter*, and, though we learn nothing specific about Zenobia's past, it is quite clear that she is not a virgin.

No novel concerned with adultery was ever less voluptuous than *The Scarlet Letter*. "To Hawthorne's imagination," says Henry James, "the fact that these two persons had loved each other too well was of an interest comparatively vulgar; what appealed to him was the idea of their moral situation in the long years that were to follow." But though the raptures of passion are not described, Hawthorne makes it perfectly clear in the great forest scene that both Hester and Dimmesdale remembered and understood them. It is not surprising that Oliver Wendell Holmes found the "rich, voluptuous, Oriental" Hester a relief from the "languid, lifeless, sexless creations" he was accustomed to encountering in American fiction.

Moreover, Hester's rich humanity is specifically rooted in her sexuality: "Her breast, with its badge of shame, was but the softer pillow for the head that needed one." Dimmesdale begins to be a man again when he stands on the scaffold beside his paramour and their child, even though as yet he can only find the courage to stand there under the cover of darkness.

The moment that he did so, there came what seemed a tumultuous rush of new life, other life than his own, pouring like a torrent into his heart, and hurrying through all his veins, as if the mother and the child were communicating their vital warmth to his half-torpid system.

From this contact he ironically derives the inspiration for his greatest sermon; from it, even more ironically, he gets the strength to repudiate the contact, to mount the scaffold at last in the sight of all men and save his soul alive.

Hawthorne seems astonishingly "modern" too in his understanding of the perversities of love. He describes the inward festering of the minister's "suppressed desires," and he knows that when the virgins of his church grow pale and tremble in his presence, it is a different passion than that which they recognize and acknowledge that moves them. He knows that love lies close to hate and that the most loving woman may resent her lover's ability to find refuge in his work from the passion which is consuming him. "Let men tremble to win the hand of woman," cries Hawthorne, "unless they win along with it the utmost passion of her heart!"

Did Hester "repent" of her sin? The question has been asked a thousand times. Whatever answer we give, we may be sure that the question would not greatly have interested her. Sin and repentance are masculine conceptions. Woman lives and builds her experience into the fabric of her days. Huckleberry Finn accepted hell to save Nigger Jim; a woman would have saved him without all the preliminary agony. Neither would she have raised the question of whether she might go to hell for it. When Hester offers to go away with Dimmesdale in the forest scene, she is hardly, from her own point of view, the temptress (though she certainly is from his); neither is she preparing for a life of self-indulgence.[5] Of course she still loves him; of course she plans to live with him. But she knows too that what he needs now is less a mistress than a nurse, and she is prepared to pay any price to give him one. She knows that if he stays where he is he will die; if she takes him away she may possibly save him. She is for the "best possible"; it hardly occurs to her to ask whether it is "right" or "wrong." It has always been woman's job to sweep up the pieces after man has finished smashing things, to salvage what she can, to dedicate herself to the continuance of life. Only men refuse to play the game unless they can formulate the rules; women have rarely had a chance to do this, and they have rarely been much interested in rules as a theoretical matter anyway. Of course it would not have worked, but that was because Dimmesdale was a man; if he could have met Hester on her own ground it would have worked. And the inevitable failure that stared her in the face was the one thing which Hester, through the mere fact of being a woman, could not have been expected to understand.

Zenobia is described with much franker emphasis upon her physical charms, though with far less sympathy. Coverdale thought it fortunate that there should be "one glimpse of a white shoulder between her gown and her kerchief." She herself threatens playfully to assume the garb of Eden after May-day, and Coverdale conjures up a picture of her in this aspect; Hawthorne toned down the passage by cutting one sentence out of it before the novel was printed.[6] Even the exotic flower in her hair typifies passion, and Coverdale is sure that "there is no folded petal, no latent dewdrop, in this perfectly developed rose!" When she is roused, he perceives her whole being "alive with a passionate intensity. . . . Any passion would have become her well; and passionate love, perhaps, the best of all."

She dies of love, but it is not because she has given herself to love that Hawthorne treats her unsympathetically. She has another fault: her mind is "full of weeds." Insofar as she is a "new woman" she has unsexed herself, and she must pay the price. She has the kind of coarseness that Hawthorne found in Margaret Fuller, upon whom he protested—not too convincingly—that he had not modeled her. That nobody may miss the point she is even made to condemn herself. It is true that Hester was also contaminated by both moral and feminist heresies during her long period of alienation from society— Hawthorne condemns her heresies without specifying them—

but there is some excuse for Hester, because society has forced an unnatural isolation upon her, and Hawthorne did not believe that one can think straight in isolation. Moreover, he condemns the Puritan punishment of her sin, not because he fails to recognize that she has sinned but because her punishment does not serve any useful purpose. The function of human law is to preserve order. Only God can judge; only God can deal with the sins of the soul. When men usurp God's functions, or thrust themselves between Him and the soul which, in Puritan modes of thinking, must ever stand naked before Him, then the order of the universe is violated, and far worse evils grow out of the very effort to set things right.[7]

Hawthorne may have been fascinated by Hester and Zenobia, but it was girls like Phoebe and Hilda [8] that he really loved, and in Phoebe's case at least it is the sexual charms over which he lingers most lovingly. He is timid enough about sex in *The House of the Seven Gables* so long as he lingers on the outskirts. Hepzibah, he awkwardly tells us, did not know what love "technically means," and he coyly refuses to observe her toilet. But there is no false modesty in his references to sexuality as an important element in Judge Pyncheon's wickedness or to its absence as an element in Clifford's deprivation. The Judge undresses Phoebe with a look ("The man, the sex, somehow or other, was entirely too prominent in the Judge's demonstrations. . . . Phoebe's eyes sank, and, without knowing why, she felt herself blushing deeply under his look"), and Clifford is hardly less sensitive to her femaleness ("He took unfailing note of every charm that appertained to her sex, and saw the ripeness of her lips, and the virginal development of her bosom"). We have heard enough nonsense about Phoebe's "commonplaceness" and "conventionality." Whatever is valid in this view was said by Hawthorne in *The House of the Seven Gables* itself long before any of his critics took up the argument. But he knew too that Phoebe is as good as bread and milk—and that those who find these commodities insipid are lost already—that she is the salt of the earth, that she has in her soul and in her body just what a man needs to cure him of his vagaries and bind him in a destiny-fulfilling way to life.

Phoebe [writes Bernard Cohen perceptively] has no aristocratic pretensions; she is a lady by nature; she needs none of the artificiality of wealth and pride to make her one. . . . She is the practical New England girl, whose economics are simple: the ability to adjust herself to any economic situation and the desire for simple means. . . . She is the only unperverted member of the Pyncheon family, and the only one with a sound sense of economics.

Hawthorne himself says, more romantically, that "she was like a prayer, offered up in the homeliest beauty of one's mother tongue." She was "a religion in herself, warm, simple, true, with a substance that could walk on earth, and a spirit that was capable of heaven."

IV

Since few men have been completely consistent in what they have felt and said about women, we should not be surprised to find Hawthorne saying both that he could talk to a responsive woman better than he could talk to any man and that he could get along well enough with men if only the women would let him alone. But certainly his writing as a whole reveals a man much more inclined to admire women than to censure them. Only "Mrs. Bullfrog" can be called a really cynical story, and this he himself gave up "to the severest reprehension" and dismissed as a stylistic experiment; "it did not come from any depth within me,—neither my heart nor my mind had anything to do with it." Even so the satire is directed as much against the man as the woman.

Love is "the one miracle . . . without which every human

existence is a blank." It is "the bliss which makes all things true, beautiful, and holy." It is also the greatest therapeutic power we know. A man who seeks perfect sympathy and understanding must look for it in a woman; he will never find it in another man. It does not matter whether the man is good or bad, mad or sane, wise or stupid. Holgrave needs Phoebe as much as the serpent-haunted Roderick Ellison needs Rosina, and if Hollingsworth ever does find salvation he finds it through Priscilla. "We will not go back," cry Josiah and Miriam, as they leave the Shaker village and set their faces toward the world of whose trials and evils they have been warned. "The world never can be dark to us, for we will always love one another." [9]

Hawthorne was not completely starry-eyed about women either. When Howells visited him at The Wayside he told him he had never seen a perfectly beautiful woman. But perhaps this was only an example of what Henry S. Kariel calls his customary "dualism of timeliness and eternity." He had previously told his journal that Nell Gwyn, as Lely depicted her in the portrait at Newstead Abbey, was "one of the few beautiful women whom I have seen on canvas"—an interesting choice for a Puritan! Hawthorne could practice what James Branch Cabell called *Domnei* with the best of them, but when he rose from his knees he knew that women were not angels. Though most of men's sunshine comes from them, he knew it was a capricious sunshine, and he was convinced too that women needed to be protected by men and guarded not only against danger but also against corruption, especially in times of crisis, which always have a tendency to shock them out of the proprieties.

Hawthorne's attitude toward George Eliot is ambiguous; we are told both that he did not wish to meet her because of the irregularity of her union with Lewes and that he attempted to get an introduction to her but failed. But his information concerning her state seems to have been vague and inaccurate,[10] and Mrs. Charles Bray says that when she met him at dinner he spent the whole time asking her questions about the novelist. Certainly Hawthorne had no fixation on sexual sins. Like Dante, and unlike many Protestants, he knew that pride and hardness of heart are worse than sensuality, but this does not mean that he "excused" the sins of the flesh any more than Dante or St. Thomas Aquinas did. In 1837 he meditated in his notebook "how much desire and resolution of doing her duty by her husband can a wife retain, while injuring him in what is deemed the most essential point?" Even raising the question made it a "liberal" sort of meditation. But the very next year he relates how an acquaintance had told him about a girl who had once confessed to him that she had been unchaste. "Mr. Leach spoke to me," he adds primly, "as if one deviation from chastity might not be an altogether insuperable objection to making a girl his wife!"

Whatever charity Hawthorne may have had for George Eliot, he had none for Margaret Fuller. He had never liked her, and in the old days, when she conducted her "Conversations" at the Peabody book shop, he had disliked Sophia's admiration for her. (He would not have been pleased if he had known that Duyckinck thought Sophia resembled her.) But there had never been any clash between them, and such contacts as they had had in Old Manse days had been pleasant. Certainly the irregularity, at its inception, of her relationship with Ossoli must have influenced the savage picture Hawthorne painted of both of them in his notebooks after their deaths, when he described Ossoli, on second-hand authority, as "entirely ignorant even of his own language, scarcely able to read at all, destitute of manners, in short, half an idiot, and without any pretensions to be a gentleman," and declared of Margaret that she had not left "in the hearts and minds of those who knew her, any deep witness of her integrity and purity."

It was such an awful joke, that she should have resolved . . . to make herself the greatest, wisest, best woman of the age; and, to that end, she set to work on her strange, heavy, unpliable, and, in many respects, defective and evil nature, and adorned it with a mosaic of admirable qualities, such as she chose to possess; putting in here a splendid talent, and there a moral excellence, and polishing each separate piece, and the whole together, till it seemed to shine afar and dazzle all who saw it. She took credit to herself for having been her own Redeemer, if not her own Creator. . . . But she was not working on inanimate substance, like marble or clay; there was something within her that she could not possibly come at, to re-create it and refine it; and, by and by, this rude old potency bestirred itself, and undid all her labor in the twinkling of an eye. On the whole, I do not know but I like her the better for it—the better, because she proved herself a very woman, after all, and fell as the weakest of her sisters might.

But it was not only the suggestion of unchastity in women that strained Hawthorne's chivalry. Ugliness, corpulence, and sometimes even old age had the same effect. If Margaret Fuller had been a more attractive woman he might well have judged her more leniently. "While he is extremely fond of a beautiful and pure woman . . ." writes William M. White, "he cares little enough for an ugly woman no matter how virtuous she might be." And he adds, severely, that "Hawthorne's squeamishness over that which is old, fat, or ugly is unwholesome." That this attitude developed very early we may infer from the shocking story of the small child's spurning a woman who tried to be kind to him: "Take her away! She is ugly and fat, and has a loud voice." Hawthorne did not need to make an effort to understand Clifford Pyncheon's weak aestheticism.

One day, before he had married Sophia, a fat woman collided with her or in some way crushed her in a public place:

I can see my Dove at this moment, my slender, little delicatest white Dove, squeezed almost out of Christendom by that great mass of female flesh—that ton of woman—that beef-eater and beer-guzzler, whose immense cloak, though broad as a ship's mainsail, could not be made to meet in front—that picture of an ale-wife —that triple, quadruple, dozen-fold old lady.

This is excusable on the basis of a lover's natural indignation, but what Hawthorne wrote about English dowagers is something else again. It seemed to him that the dreadnaught type of woman was much commoner in England than at home, and indeed that Englishwomen were "capable of being more atrociously ugly than any other human beings." In *Our Old Home* he published this opinion to the world, and surely English readers were justified in their indignation. It is amazing to find Fields writing him, after this material had come out in the *Atlantic,* that friends had stopped him in the street to laugh over this very matter. Evidently the famous nineteenth-century squeamishness in matters of taste was of a highly selective variety.

I have heard a good deal of the tenacity with which English ladies retain their personal beauty to a late period of life; but (not to suggest that an American eye needs use and cultivation before it can quite appreciate the charm of English beauty at any age) it strikes me that an English lady of fifty is apt to become a creature less refined and delicate, so far as her physique goes, than anything that we Western people class under the name of woman. She has an awful ponderosity of frame, not pulpy, like the looser development of our few fat women, but massive with solid beef and streaky tallow: so that (though struggling manfully against the idea) you inevitably think of her as made of steaks and sirloins. When she walks her advance is elephantine. When she sits down, it is on a great round space of her Maker's footstool, where she looks as if nothing could ever move her. . . .

You can meet this figure in the street, and live, and even smile at the recollection. But conceive of her in a ball-room, with the bare, brawny arms that she invariably displays there, and all the other corresponding development, such as is beautiful in the maiden blossom, but a spectacle to howl at in such an overblown cabbage-rose as this. . . .

It is a pity that the English violet should grow into such an outrageously developed peony. . . . I wonder whether a middle-aged husband ought to be considered as legally married to all the accretions that have overgrown the slenderness of his bride, since he led her to the altar, and which make her so much more than he ever bargained for! Is it not a sounder view of the case, that the matrimonial bond cannot be held to include the three fourths of the wife that had no existence when the ceremony was performed? And as matter of conscience and good morals, ought not an English married pair to insist upon the celebration of a silver wedding at the end of twenty-five years, in order to legalize and mutually appropriate that corporeal growth of which both parties have individually come into possession since they were pronounced one flesh?

In his notebooks he was even more savage about these "grim, red-faced monsters." "Surely, a man would be justified in murdering them—in taking a sharp knife and cutting away their mountainous flesh, until he had brought them into reasonable shape."

Hawthorne also disliked what we call "career women." He realized the hard lot of women yoked to unworthy men and recognized the cruelty of putting half the race into a position where if they failed in love they failed in life, with no resource open to them except needlework or opening a cent shop like Hepzibah Pyncheon's. He could even see that a woman's point of view might be valuable in legislation, and he knew that a woman's impressions of public men are often penetrating. In Rome he showed himself surprisingly tolerant of women like Harriet Hosmer and Louisa Lander, who lived as independently as men and quite without censure. But in the last analysis his heart was with the needlework, and it was not only in Hester's case that he invested it with all sorts of spiritual significance.

One might suppose that if a woman could devote herself to any occupation without being subjected to coarsening contacts with a corrupt world, it would be writing. But Hawthorne hated women writers. "America is now wholly given over to a damned mob of scribbling women," he wrote Ticknor in 1855, "and I should have no chance of success while the public taste is occupied with their trash—and should be ashamed of myself if I did succeed." To Fields he wrote even more savagely, "*All* women, as authors, are feeble and tiresome. I wish they were forbidden to write, on pain of having their faces deeply scarified with an oyster-shell."

There were a number of reasons for this feeling. The one least creditable to Hawthorne was that the success of women writers outraged his masculine vanity: the husbands of celebrated women, he says, are generally insignificant men. Among the "damned mob of scribbling women" who achieved success there were few whose talents he respected, and he would not have been human had he not resented Maria Cummins or Elizabeth Wetherell making so much more money out of literature than he was able to make.

But this was the factor that influenced him least. He did not believe women qualified either by native endowment or by training to write first-rate books, and, insofar as they preempted the field, he believed that literature itself must suffer. Moreover, he saw literature as an opening wedge for woman's entrance into other fields where she would be even more hopelessly out of place: this he shows clearly when he opens his paper on Anne Hutchinson with an attack on female writers.

Even Queen Elizabeth and Queen Christina were in his eyes too manlike. "Women are too good for authorship, and that is the reason it spoils them so." Pursuing it, they must lose more than they gain. Even when such genius is present that the woman has no choice but express it, she must still expect to pay a price.

Authorship, like all the arts, does undoubtedly encourage —and require—a kind of spiritual nudism, and an age which was shocked by women's bodies could hardly have been expected not to shudder over a naked mind. Hawthorne himself says that writing has "pretty much the same effect" on women "as it would to walk through the streets physically stark naked." He himself shuddered even when the work seemed to him good. When Ticknor sent him Julia Ward Howe's *Passion Flowers* in 1854 he wrote:

Those are admirable poems of Mrs. Howe's, but the devil must be in the woman to publish them. It seems to me to let out a whole history of domestic unhappiness. What a strange propensity it is in these scribbling women to make a show of their hearts, as well as their heads, upon your counter, for anybody to pry into that chooses! However, I, for one, am much obliged to the lady, and esteem her beyond comparison the first of American poetesses. What does her husband think of it?

Three years later, rejecting *Leonora*, he is still harping on the same string:

I read her play, (and thank you for it,) but her genius does not appear to be of the dramatic order. In fact, she has no genius or talent, except for making public what she ought to keep to herself —viz. her passions, emotions, and womanly weaknesses. "Passion Flowers" were delightful; but she ought to have been soundly whipped for publishing them.

And if Mrs. Howe deserved whipping there were other women who deserved something worse:

In Grace Greenwood's last "Little Pilgrim," there is a description of her new baby!!! in response to numerous inquiries which, she says, have been received from her subscribers. I wonder she did not think it necessary to be brought to bed in public, or, at least, in presence of a committee of the subscribers. My dearest, I cannot enough thank God that, with a higher and deeper intellect than any other woman, thou hast never—forgive me the base idea! —prostituted thyself to the public, as that woman has, and as a thousand others do. It does seem to me to deprive women of all delicacy.

Yet, oddly enough, when Fields wanted Mrs. Hawthorne to contribute to the *Atlantic*, her husband merely remarked mildly, "I have never read anything so good as some of her narrative and descriptive epistles to her friends." She did not contribute to the *Atlantic*, though she did publish her *Notes on England and Italy* five years after Hawthorne's death. On the other hand, when he overheard little Rose tell a companion that she was writing stories, he was furious. "Never let me hear of your writing stories!" he cried. "I forbid you to write them."

Here again, since Hawthorne was human, we ought not to look for a perfect consistency. Perhaps his admiration for Gail Hamilton might be dismissed as the exception that proves the rule. "My wife likes her hugely, and for my part, I had no idea that there was such a sensible woman of letters in the world. She is just as healthy-minded as if she had never touched a pen." But what about Delia Bacon? If any woman ever made a spectacle of herself through publishing a book it was she, yet Hawthorne stood her sponsor. When George William Curtis was trying to build a magazine, Hawthorne advised him to rely upon young writers and did not draw any distinction as to sex. "There is a woman somewhere in the West—I forget her name; but she wrote an article called the 'Age of Jonathan' for the gold medal of the Albany Female Academy in 1850

—who is bound to shine in our literature. You had better hunt her up, and engage her." And sometimes, like other people, he could be perverse. Mrs. Mowatt's plays he found "silly enough to be pleasant reading," and he exempted Fanny Fern from his general condemnation of ink-stained women for the very reason that she was a pre-eminent embodiment of all the faults he most disliked; Fanny Fern, he said, wrote as if the devil were in her.

Generally women write like emasculated men, and are only to be distinguished from male authors by greater feebleness and folly; but when they throw off the restraints of decency, and come before the public stark naked, as it were—then their books are sure to possess character and value.

V

When the Hawthornes were married on July 9, 1842, Sophia Peabody was approaching her thirty-third birthday,[11] and her husband had just passed his thirty-eighth. The daughter of a dentist and homeopathic physician of Boston and Salem, she was already well read, a good linguist, and a capable artist. Her horizon had been enlarged by an extended stay in Cuba, during which she had kept a voluminous journal. She had also suffered for years from dreadful and constant headaches, which her mother believed had exercised a beneficial effect upon her character.

Ada Shepard did not think Sophia at all beautiful, and Julian Hawthorne seems to agree in a technical sense, though he adds that in her presence nobody would have thought of raising the question. Though twentieth-century readers sometimes find Sophia's aspiring idealism hard to take and call her letters "gushing," she was far more realistic, and much less inclined to extremism, than either of her sisters. When she bowdlerized her husband's letters and journals after his death, she sinned against the canons of perfect scholarship; that she also sinned against him is rather more than doubtful. If we study Hawthorne's own editing of the similar materials which he himself prepared for the press, we may well be convinced that, had he lived to do the job she did for him, he might well have made many, though not all, of her changes. As a matter of fact, either one of them would have experienced some difficulty in getting the materials published in their time on any other basis.

Adult contact between the Peabodys and the Hawthornes (they had lived near each other in Salem since childhood) was brought about through Elizabeth's interest in Hawthorne's tales. The first time Hawthorne called on the Peabodys with his sisters the invalid Sophia was in her chamber. Elizabeth ran upstairs at the earliest opportunity, urging her sister to dress and come down to meet a visitor "handsomer than Lord Byron," but Sophia only laughed, saying that if he had called once he would call again. He did, and it was upon this occasion that the two first stood face to face. The mutual attraction was overwhelming and instantaneous, but he looked at her so intently that he frightened her. The evening ended with Elizabeth's promise to call at the Hawthorne house, but Sophia declined the invitation on the ground that she never went out in the evening. " 'I wish you would!' he said, in a low, urgent tone. But she smiled, and shook her head, and he went away."

They soon progressed beyond this, however, and it was not long before each understood how the other felt. But there were two great barriers between them. One was Hawthorne's poverty, and the other was Sophia's health. The latter they agreed to leave to God. If it was His will that Sophia should marry Nathaniel, He would relieve her of her headaches. God graciously vouchsafed the sign. Apparently they did not ask Him for money; in any case He did not send any. But in spite of this and all other difficulties they were united at last.

Their life at the Old Manse has again and again been called Edenic, and the figure is not misplaced; after more than a century it still warms the heart and renews faith in life to know that one man and one woman learned how good living and loving can be.

It is as if the original relation between Man and Nature were restored in my case, and that I were to look exclusively to her for the support of my Eve and myself—to trust to her for food and clothing, and all things needful, with the full assurance that she could not fail me. The fight with the world—the struggle of a man among men—the agony of the universal effort to wrench the means of life from a host of greedy competitors—all this seems like a dream to me. My business is merely to live and to enjoy; and whatever is essential to life and enjoyment will come as naturally as the dew from Heaven. This is—practically, at least, my faith.

Then the old New England conscience stirs and pricks but it is soon pacified: "True, it might be a sin and a shame, in such a world as ours, to spend a life-time in this manner; but, for a few summer weeks, it is good to live as if this world were Heaven."

"I have married the Spring!" he cries. "I am husband to the month of May!" She tells him to burn a portion of one of her letters but he cannot do it, "for never was a wife's deep, warm, chaste love so well expressed, and it is as holy to me as the Bible. Oh, I cannot begin to tell thee how I love thee." Yet there were times when they thought they might safely dispense with speech altogether. "We have soared into a region where we talk together in a language that can have no earthly echo."

He can no longer *see* without her. "Had my wife been with

me, I should have had a far deeper sense of beauty; for I should have looked through the medium of her spirit." Nor can he *be seen*, for when Longfellow invites him to Cambridge to meet his brother Stephen again and renew their memories of college days, he declines and invites Stephen to Concord instead. "If I were to come to Cambridge, he would see but the smallest portion of me—here, he will find me extant in a threefold capacity, my wife and little girl making up the complete individual." It was a union for time and Eternity, and he was content to give both into her keeping:

If you fail me (but there is no such if) I might toil onward through this life without much outward change, but I should sink down and die utterly upon the threshold of the dreary Future. Were *you* to find yourself deceived, you would betake yourself at once to God and Heaven, in the certainty of there finding a thousand-fold recompense for all earthly disappointment; but with me, it seems as if hope and happiness would be torn up by the roots, and could never bloom again, neither in this soil nor in the soil of Paradise.

When his wife left him to go to Boston and visit her sister, he helped her into the "wagon" which came for her "and stood watching her, on the door-step, till she was out of sight. Then I betook myself to sawing and splitting wood; there being an inward unquietness, which demanded active exercise, and I sawed, I think, more briskly than ever before." After dinner he lay down "with the Devil in my heart, and attempted to sleep; but sleep would not come,—for the sufficient reason, perhaps, that my little wife was at that very moment jolting most uncomfortably over a rough road." When a letter came he "read, and re-read, and re-re-read, and quadruply, quintuply, and sextuply re-read, . . . until I had it all by heart; and then continued to re-read it for the sake of looking at the fairy penmanship." He wanted her to "know my life, during our separation, as circumstancially as if thou hadst been all the time by my side." Yet he knew it was no good, for not only had all pleasures disappeared, but the very necessities had lost their savor. He was even ashamed to eat alone; "it becomes the mere gratification of animal appetite—the tribute which we are compelled to pay to our grosser nature; whereas, in thy company, it is refined, and moralized, and spiritualized."

He never changed about these things; when he was left alone in Liverpool in the 'fifties his tone was quite the same. And Mrs. Hawthorne's tone matched or surpassed his own. Just before her marriage she described him as looking "like the angel of the Apocalypse, so powerful and gentle. It seems as if I were realizing the dreams of the poets in my own person." A month after marriage, he was "the loveliest being who ever breathed life. Yes, with all his strength and spirit and power, he has the most perfect loveliness of nature I ever witnessed or imagined." Even the vegetables he raised were delicious beyond all comparison with others. "When Apollos tend herds and till the earth, it is but reasonable to expect unusual effects." And she cries: "Oh lovely GOD! I thank Thee that I can rush to my husband with all my many waters, and sing and thunder with all my waves in the vast expanse of his comprehension. How I exult there—how I foam and sparkle in the Sun of his love—how I wish for no broader region, because I have as yet found no limit to this."

But the Hawthornes had one kind of trouble that Adam and Eve did not know. They both had in-laws. Hawthorne never extended his notion of Sophia's perfections to her family. The very day after arriving at the Old Manse he wrote his sister Louisa that "in taking to myself a wife, I have neither given up my own relatives nor adopted others." Many young wives would have been hurt by the kind of letter Hawthorne sent Sophia in 1844:

> I called at the book room in Boston, and saw there thy mother, thy brother Nat, and Elizabeth!!—besides two or three ladies. It was the most awkward place in the world to talk about Una and other kindred subjects; so I made my escape as soon as possible, promising to return to dine if convenient, and resolving that it should be as inconvenient as possible.

Sophia probably was not hurt, for as early as the time she lived in Lenox she became a sufficiently dutiful wife to be able to write to tell her father he must not make so long a visit again; he had disturbed "Mr. Hawthorne." Consider, too, Elizabeth's position. She had admired Hawthorne before Sophia did, and it was she who had brought them together. But her abolitionism (and Mary's too) and her generally high and dry point of view strained the ties between her and her brother-in-law increasingly as time went on, and the ties with her sister also, for whenever there was a difference of opinion Sophia sided with him. Some of Hawthorne's letters to Elizabeth are more than a little sharp, as when he reproached her with her "awful squint" on abolition—"and it is queer, though natural, that you think everybody squints, except yourself" —or indicates that "the conjugal relation" being "one which God never meant you to share, and which therefore He apparently did not give you the instinct to understand"—why, she might at least refrain from giving advice to those who did understand it. Hawthorne did not trouble to keep his friends ignorant of his attitude toward his sister-in-law either:

> I enclose a letter to E. P. Peabody [he wrote Ticknor from England in 1856], and I particularly wish that you will learn her present direction, and forward it without delay. She has taken it into her head that Mrs. Hawthorne is extremely ill; and unless prevented seasonably, I shall expect to see her on this side of the

water. This would be exceedingly awkward and inconvenient; moreover, Mrs. Hawthorne is better, at this moment, than at any time since the first six months of her residence in England.

Poor Elizabeth! She was telling the whole human race how to run its affairs. It must have been hard to be debarred as adviser in her own sister's family.

Hawthorne did not think his own family perfect either. Horace Conolly says, if we can believe him, that Hawthorne once declared he didn't "wish to look like any Hawthorne." Yet for all the reserve that prevailed in the Hawthorne household, its members were attached to each other, or as he himself puts it in an 1842 letter to Louisa, "Believe me (not the less because I seldom say it) your very loving brother." He may have loved Louisa more than he loved his older sister Elizabeth, who was closer to him intellectually, but he could rebuke either one of them when he thought she deserved it, as in reporting Rose's birth to Louisa: "Judging by your long silence, you will not take much interest in the intelligence, nor in anything else which concerns us. I should really like to hear from you once or twice in the course of a twelvemonth." And Mrs. Hawthorne invited Louisa to visit them very early in their married life, "because I wanted her to know that her worshipped brother is not very miserable with me." Another invitation to Louisa, ten years later, had tragic overtones, for she was on her way to Concord when she was killed in a terrible Hudson River steamboat accident. Hawthorne had hoped that this time she would stay, and when the news came he went off by himself even from Sophia to try to adjust himself to it.

"The only thing I fear," Hawthorne had once written, "is the ridicule of Elizabeth." Perhaps she was too close to him to want another woman to come closer. At least we hear that she opposed his engagement and delayed communicating the news to his mother on the ground that the shock "would kill her," which is hard to believe of the woman who wrote the wise, sensible, and highly intelligent letters which the Hawthorne children received for so many years.[12] It is delightful to know that when at last Madame Hawthorne was told, she was neither killed nor surprised, for the excellent reason that, being a perceptive woman, she had suspected it all along. Later there was trouble with Elizabeth over Una, when she not only fed the child with sweetmeats behind her parents' backs but even tried to corrupt her by telling her that her mother need never know. "Elizabeth," writes Sophia in another connection, with as close an approach to bitterness as was possible for her, "is not available for every-day purposes of pot-hooks and trammels, spits and float-irons."

At this time Hawthorne and Sophia were living in the same house with his family at Salem but in separate apartments, this being the only condition under which Hawthorne felt justified in asking Sophia to live there and the only one under which he thought it tolerable for himself. The relative seclusion which the several persons involved managed to secure in a small house was wonderful, but when Madame Hawthorne lay dying, it was Sophia, rather than her own daughters, to whom she turned. This was a difficult time for Hawthorne, and it seems to have been an illuminating one too:

At about five o'clock I went to my mother's chamber, and was shocked to see such an alteration since my last visit. I love my mother; but there has been, ever since boyhood, a sort of coldness of intercourse between us. . . . I did not expect to be much moved at the time,—that is to say, not to feel any overpowering emotion struggling just then—though I knew that I should deeply remember and regret her. . . . She knew me, but could only murmur a few indistinct words; among which I understand an injunction to take care of my sisters. Mrs. Dike left the chamber, and then I found the tears slowly gathering in my eyes. I tried to keep them down, but it would not be; I kept filling up, till, for a few moments,

I shook with sobs. For a long time I knelt there, holding her hand; and surely it is the darkest hour I ever lived. Afterwards I stood by the open window and looked through the crevice of the curtain. The shouts, laughter, and cries of the two children had come up into the chamber from the open air, making a strange contrast with the death-bed scene. And now, through the crevice of the curtain, I saw my little Una of the golden locks, looking very beautiful, and so full of spirit and life that she was life itself. And then I looked at my poor dying mother, and seemed to see the whole of human existence at once, standing in the dusty midst of it.

Nobody has ever questioned the element of exaltation in Hawthorne's love for Sophia. He looked upon their union as having been made in Eternity; he stood in awe of his wife as if in the presence of a spirit. "She is a flower to be worn in no man's bosom, but was sent from Heaven to show the possibilities of the human soul."

Unfortunately it has not always been recognized that Hawthorne also loved Sophia with a man's passion, and that there was no conflict in his mind between his sexual and his spiritual needs. No man was ever freer of that perverted puritanism or platonism (to give a fancy name to a very ugly abnormality), which, denying clean passion, produces the very evils it pretends to deplore. Distinguishing between the sexuality of Milton's Adam and Eve before and after the Fall, C. S. Lewis has remarked that since we live in a fallen world none of us has ever experienced unfallen sexuality. If anybody since the Fall has, it must have been Hawthorne and Sophia. They regarded themselves as united eternally long before their wedding day; if their bodies could not come together their imaginations could; in their private correspondence the betrothed were "husband" and "wife" to each other.

My own wife, what a cold night this is going to be! How I am to keep warm, unless you nestle close, close into my bosom, I do not by any means understand—not but what I have clothes enough on my mattress—but a husband cannot be comfortably warm without his wife.[13]

Sophia might have been offended by such freedom, indeed must have been if she had been what many persons believe New England girls to have been during this period. But she was not offended. What an injustice she did to herself when she deleted such passages as this in her editing of Hawthorne's memorabilia, yet how could she possibly have done anything else? "Oh, how happy you make me by calling me your husband—by subscribing yourself my wife. I kiss that word when I meet it in your letters; and I repeat over and over to myself, 'she is my wife—I am her husband.' "

After hard, cruel waiting they reached Eden-in-Concord at last, and then they no longer needed to play husband and wife on paper. "Then came my dear little wife to her husband; which is more than can be said of every wife in the world." One Sunday they were even (as we should say) "petting" in the parlor when Margaret Fuller called, and "Sophia 'sprang from her husband's embrace' wondering if her hair were completely disheveled and whether her face were as pink as it felt." [14] But from that time until the end they knew the old agonies only when they were separated, which fortunately was not often. "Oh, my wife, I do want thee so intolerably. Nothing else is real, except the bond between thee and me. The people around me are but shadows. I am myself but a shadow, till thou takest me in thy arms, and convertest me into substance. Till thou comest back, I do but walk in a dream."

All this is true, but to stop here would be misleading, and here we return to the difference between fallen and unfallen sexuality. Fallen sexuality, I should say, is sexuality which fails to relate itself properly and reasonably and realistically to the other aspects, claims, and interests of life, and which uses its partner for the gratification of personal passion without proper regard to his dignity as a human being and as a child of God. During the last year of her life Sophia Hawthorne told her sister Elizabeth that her husband "so respected" her "delicacy of constitution . . . that he proposed they should have but three children, and that there should be two and a half years between the first two, and five years between the second and third." She added, somewhat startlingly, that "Mr. Hawthorne's passions were under his feet." [15] The frankness of this confidence may have been less rare than we imagine among nineteenth-century ladies, but the self-control suggested must surely be rare in any period. "I have not been well in the body," wrote Sophia in the journal she and her husband kept jointly during their first year of marriage, "so that I could not be so demonstrative as usual, but there is never any variation in my felicity, while I recognize my position, and know that I am indeed his wife."

But with all this ecstasy and idealism there was mingled in both the Hawthornes a sure, dependable fund of common sense. They worshipped each other but they also understood each other, and neither asked more of the other than it was in his nature to give. During their engagement Sophia could not even get this "most unmalleable man," as he calls himself, to go to hear the great seaman's preacher, Father Taylor, whom such distinguished visitors as Dickens and Jenny Lind regarded as one of the sights of Boston. She did not have much more success in getting him to listen to Emerson, and neither Sophia nor her family ever made a Transcendentalist of Hawthorne; he came much closer to detranscendentalizing her. The Hawthornes respected each other's integrity, and they respected each other's reserves. Few writers have had wives who understood and appreciated their work better; none ever had a wife who more completely and cordially accepted the fact that it was his work and not hers, and that he and not she must decide what was going into it.[16]

Was he, then, the dominating partner in their marriage? I do not see how there can be any question about it. He had dominated his mother and his sisters before marriage, and I think he carried the same habit into his new home. Even his desire to protect his wife led him in this direction:

Dearest, I never think you to blame; for you positively have no faults. Not that you always act wisely, or judge wisely, or feel precisely what it would be wise to feel, in relation to this present world and state of being; but it is because you are too delicately and exquisitely wrought in heart, mind, and frame, to dwell in such a world—because, in short, you are fitter to be in Paradise than here. . . . Were an angel, however holy and wise, to come and dwell with mortals, he would need the guidance and instruction of some mortal; and so will you, my Dove, need mine—and precisely the same sort of guidance that the angel would.

Julian makes the interesting statement that Hawthorne deferred to Sophia when he was in doubt. But he was often sure, even in purely domestic matters.

He never lets me get tired [so Sophia wrote her mother in 1846]. He arrests me the moment before I do too much, and he is then immitigable; and I cannot obtain grace to sew even an inch more, even if an inch would finish my work. I have such rich experience of his wisdom in these things, that whatever may be the inconvenience, I gracefully submit.

This, of course, was "loving care," but even loving care can be trying when it is "immitigable." He ruled over her clothes too:

The dark purple mousseline which I wore in Boston I have had to give up; for my husband all at once protested that he *could not see me* in it any longer, and that he hated it beyond all endurance. . . . Mr. Hawthorne does not like to see me wear dark materials, and he is truly contented only when I shine in silk.

Rose could not wear a hat with a high crown either because he said it make her look like a Lieutenant General and made him afraid of her. But when Sophia made him a really gorgeous dressing gown—"the ground-work was purple, covered all over with the conventional palm-leaf in old-gold color; the lining was red"—he at once began wiping his pen on the lining, and, instead of remonstrating, Sophia simply sewed a pen-wiper in the shape of a butterfly on the soiled place. It will not do to make too much of these things, for Hawthorne was a most loving husband. But it will not do to leave them out altogether either.

A very important element in Hawthorne's opposition to Sophia's proposed use of mesmerism to cure her headaches in the early days was his inability to endure the thought of another person establishing a control over her mind which he was not able to share, and once at least he seems to have extended this particular kind of jealousy to embrace the dead. In 1858, when Sophia was in Lisbon, news came to Hawthorne in Liverpool of the death of O'Sullivan's brother. "Do not sympathize too much," he wrote her. "Thou art wholly mine, and must not overburden thyself with anybody's grief—not even that of thy dearest friend next to me." Here, again, I would not make too much of this, but the statement is at least suggestive.

The one peculiarity in the Hawthornes' domestic arrangements was their—and particularly his—attitude toward domestic chores. He seems to have shared with Longfellow the curious idea that cooking somehow degraded a woman. "I never in my life saw my mother cook anything," writes her younger daughter. "It was my father's desire that she never should." Women with many times Sophia Hawthorne's money at their disposal nowadays perform daily many tasks that she considered beneath her, and few of them are able to spend a full hour each morning brushing their hair, as we are told she did. Poor as the Hawthornes were when they went to the Old Manse, they had an Irish girl to "do" for them, and when they could no longer afford to keep Mary Brian, it was Hawthorne, not Sophia, who took over.

He rose betimes in the mornings, and kindled fires in the kitchen and breakfast room, and by the time I came down, the tea-kettle boiled, and potatoes were baked and rice cooked, and my lord sat with a book, superintending. Just imagine that superb head peeping at the rice or examining the potatoes with the air and port of a monarch!

However little there was to eat, it must always be served off "the finest French china," since it was inconceivable to Mrs. Hawthorne that her "*second-best* services" should be used for her "most illustrious guest," her husband.

But alas! again for the inconsistencies of the human animal:

The avenue is strewed with withered leaves—the whole crop, apparently, of last year, some of which my wife had raked into heaps, intending to make a bonfire of them. I wonder what becomes of them, when there is no "neat-handed Phillis" to sweep them away.

What indeed! It was clear they need not look to Corydon. For if Phillis could rake but not cook, then Corydon would cook but not rake.

VI

Besides being a good and loving husband Hawthorne was a good and loving father. From the time he stopped writing each day until bedtime he was with his wife and children, playing games and making wonderful playthings, reading aloud and telling wonderful stories, though Rose does say that she had less of society than the other children who had come along before he was famous. "At noon papa descends from his study," writes Sophia of one occasion, "instead of at night; and this causes great rejoicing throughout his kingdom." They were not supposed to intrude upon him while he was working, but like other children they did not always do what they were supposed to do, and he does not seem to have been rigid about it. Once he even put in an appearance at a children's party at The Wayside and was quite the lion of the affair, though it is clear that unfamiliarity and a sense of awe were large elements in his success.

The characteristic, odd, even amazing thing about Hawthorne in his relationship to his children, however, is that there is no trace whatever of the romanticizing or idealizing imagination that operated upon his wife. No reader of "The Snow Image" needs to be reminded that Hawthorne understood what Wordsworth meant when he postulated and celebrated a quality of spiritual insight in children. This appears too in *Grandfather's Chair:* "Often, in a young child's ideas and fancies, there is something that it requires the thought of a lifetime to comprehend." Hawthorne composed even so trifling a work as his *Biographical Stories* with "a deep sense of responsibility. The Author regards children as sacred, and would not, for the world, cast anything into the fountain of a young heart that might embitter and pollute its waters."

But he did know, clearly, that those waters are capable of pollution, and F. O. Matthiessen has compared the depraved children of "The Gentle Boy," who torture Ilbrahim, with the depraved children of "The Turn of the Screw." This is soundly observed, but Hawthorne reminds me much more of a great recent writer who knew far more about children than James did (and who, incidentally, greatly admired Hawthorne)— I mean the Walter de la Mare of such stories as "The Trumpet" and "An Ideal Craftsman." Hawthorne was not, in the de la Mare sense, a specialist in children, yet some of the notations he has left us on the behavior of his own children —Una in particular—approach the clinical. In her father's eyes, Una's beauty was transitory, evanescent, and unaccountable; "if you glance sideways at her, you perhaps think it is illuminating her face, but, turning full round to enjoy, it is gone again." Her mouth was "a kind of miracle; it does not look large, yet it is capable of extending to an unimaginable width, and of receiving mouthfuls that would startle an ogre;—a trait of which I have just been reminded by seeing her eat an apple." Hawthorne may not go quite so far as J. M. Barrie, who found children "heartless," but he did know that the sympathies of childhood are at best "fitful." So Una's conduct was "elfish or angelic" depending on how one looked at it "but, at all events, supernatural. . . . In short, I now and then catch an aspect in her in which I cannot believe her to be my own human child, but a spirit strangely mingled with good and evil, haunting the house where I dwell." And if it be objected that this *is* imaginative, I can only reply that, by the same token, it is not wholly admiring.

In *Dr. Grimshawe's Secret* Hawthorne recognizes that there are people to whom loving their children does not come naturally, and he thinks the reason may be that these persons do not love themselves: "they shrink from their own features in the reflection presented in these little mirrors." It was his opinion that he himself had no "natural partiality" for his children. "I love them according to their deserts—they have to prove their claim to all the affection they get; and I believe I could love other people's children better than mine, if I felt that they deserved it more."

Most utterances of this kind can be dismissed on the ground that the speaker deceived himself. I am not so sure about

Hawthorne. Consider the following extracts from letters to Sophia, and note the progression involved:

December 2, 1844: I long to see our little Una; but she is not yet a vital portion of my being. I find that her idea merges in thine. I wish for thee; and our daughter is included in that wish, without being particularly expressed.

December 20, 1844: Also, I love our little Una—and, I think, with much more adequate comprehension of her loveliness, than before we left Concord.

November 13, 1845: [As] for me, I already love the future little personage; and yet, somehow or other, I feel a jealousy of him or her, on Una's account, and should not choose to have the new baby better than the old one.

March 15, 1847: I love thee infinitely, and need thee constantly. I long to hear Una's voice. I find that I even love Bundlebreech!!!

"Bundlebreech," of course, was the new baby, Julian. To the displeasure of his own austere relatives, Hawthorne had given his first child a "fancy" and idealistic name out of *The Faerie Queene* and then addressed her as "Onion." And it is said that Mrs. Hawthorne might have named her Louise, except that she feared her husband might make it "Louse."

Julian had a harder time than Una in finding his way into his father's heart, for Julian had the misfortune to be a boy. Hawthorne's relations with children during his bachelorhood are not without charm; he had been much devoted to the little daughter of his cousin Nancy Forrester Barstow, and we hear about delightful stories told to children even in very early days; but the child is always a girl, never a boy. Boys, he told his sister Elizabeth, were not worth raising. He "raised" Julian; he even "raised" him lovingly and with care; but there may be some question as to whether he really changed his mind. Julian, who was seventeen when his father died, said that they "never had any serious man-and-boy talks together," a circumstance which he generously attributed to his being "in most ways juvenile for my age." It may not have been wholly on that account, however. There is no better example of Mrs. Hawthorne's astonishing capacity to take her husband as she found him than her frank, untroubled, and quite rancorless statement about Julian to Horatio Bridge: "His father declares he does not care anything about him because he is a boy, and so I am obliged to love him twice as much as I otherwise should."

Once more, these remarks cannot be taken literally. No father could have been kinder to a boy than Hawthorne was to Julian, or taken better care of him when he was left in his charge. But again let us glance at Hawthorne's diaries:

February 1, 1849: He is truly a happy little soul, if ever one there were on earth; and, for his sake, I am more inclined to think the race of man was not created in bitterness, and for their misery, but in infinite benevolence, and for eternal blessedness.

August 10, 1851: Let me say outright, for once, that he is a sweet and lovely little boy, and worthy of all the love I am capable of giving him. Thank God! Bless him! God bless Phoebe [Sophia] for giving him to me! God bless her as the best wife and mother in the world! God bless Una, whom I long to see again! God bless little Rosebud! God bless me, for Phoebe's and all their sakes! No other man has so good a wife; nobody has better children. Would I were worthier of her and them!

November 3, 1855: He is really a great comfort and joy to me, and rather unexpectedly so; for I must confess that I wished to keep him here on his own account and thine [Sophia's], much more than on my own.

April 7, 1856: The old boy writes to me in the best of spirits; and I rather think he can do without me better than I can without him; for I really find I love him a *little*, and that his society is one of my necessities. . . .

There is affection here, but, making all allowances for playfulness, there is to my ear a kind of condescension too, and we must not forget that as late as 1858 Hawthorne was also remarking that "all boys are the awkwardest and unbeautifullest creatures whom God has made." When Una went to stay with the Fieldses her father wrote, "I hope you like her. We do." But Julian? "I hope Julian's visit has not bored you intolerably. It is certainly a relief to get rid of him occasionally; he is too big for a small house. Don't tell him so, however."

Even with the girls, however, the note of oddity does not quite disappear. There can be no question as to Hawthorne's suffering over Una when she was critically ill in Rome; indeed his wife felt that he never got over it. "Even when he looks at his Rose of Sharon—so firm and strong now, I think he feels uncertain that she still lives and blooms, so deeply scored into his soul was the expectation of her death. It was his first acquaintance with suffering, and it seemed to rend him asunder." But what are we to make of Julian's statement, made apparently upon his mother's authority, that the grief Hawthorne "felt at the idea that perhaps his daughter might die was so keen that he could not endure the alternations of hope and fear, and therefore had settled with himself not to hope at all"? And Maria Mitchell recorded that on Una's sixteenth birthday, which would be on March 3, 1860, or less than a year and a half after her illness had first struck her, Hawthorne drank her health in cold water and said, "May you live happily, and be ready to go when you must," an almost incredibly inconsiderate and tactless action, if correctly reported, which I should have expected of the *memento mori* type of religious fanatic but not of Hawthorne.

CHAPTER SIX

GOD'S CHILD

I

A man's religion ought to give meaning to all his other interests and activities and provide a frame of reference for them. If it does not, he can hardly be said to have a religion. Hawthorne's indifference to the church as an institution has prevented many readers from understanding that he had a religion. "Shall you want me to be a minister, Doctor or Lawyer?" he asked his mother in 1820; then quickly added, "A minister I will not be." It is generally assumed that he did not attend church at all after he grew up, and this was practically, though not literally, true. He did not join the missionary society at Bowdoin, yet he seems distressed over the neglect of religion at college. In "Main Street" he wonders why one who might worship God "beneath the awful vault of the firmament" should look for him in the "pent-up nook" of a church. In "Sunday at Home" he acknowledges the holiness of the Sabbath light—so long as it endured man need not despair of the world—but he made it clear that he himself participated in the service vicariously.

The reverend clergy did not tend to make the church attractive to him. Their gloom oppressed him; their geniality was worse since it seemed professional, hypocritical, put on and off like a clerical costume. As a small child he so hated a bust of Wesley he found in the house that he filled it up with water and put it in a cold place in the hope that it would burst.

He hated the portraits of his clerical predecessors at the Old Manse too, and he was sure he would have hated the sermons they left behind them if he had been unfortunate enough to have to read them. "I find that my respect for clerical people, as such, and my faith in the utility of their office, decreases daily," he wrote in 1842. "We certainly do need a new revelation—a new system—for there seems to be no life in the old one."

In England the situation altered somewhat. Consul Hawthorne took a pew for his family in W. H. Channing's Unitarian Church at Liverpool, but he does not seem to have occupied it often. In 1853 Sophia writes (inaccurately) [1] that the children have never yet been to church and rejoices that they are to have their first experience in the beautiful Chester Cathedral. Though she herself considered the Church of England "the merest petrifaction," not having "the fervor and unction of the Roman Catholic even," she was "deeply" affected by the service. But both Una and Julian were bored by the sermon, Julian once yawning aloud, "which so startled Mr. Hawthorne that he exclaimed, '*Good God!*' thus making the matter much worse." Hawthorne himself seems to have found religious inspiration only in the architecture of the English churches. Ritual meant nothing to him, and he thought the sermon "puny" even in Westminster Abbey. He may not have had much relish for sermons, but he was still a good enough New Englander to feel that if you do go to church the preaching of the Word should dominate. He did somewhat better with the family prayers he was now expected to conduct as head of a dignified and official household—he had always thought well of grace before meat—and, though he once remarked that the English "bring themselves no nearer to God when they pray, than when they play at cards," Julian thought he officiated very impressively.

In a measure Hawthorne may even be said to have become a preacher himself in England, and like Ernest of "The Great Stone Face" he achieved this office "almost involuntarily." "When I used to sit in his office in the Liverpool consulate," wrote Julian, "I sometimes heard him speak plain truths to the waifs and strays who drifted in there; and truth more plain, yet bestowed with more humanity and brotherly purpose, I have never heard since." His most illustrious victim—or bene-ficiary—was the American Doctor of Divinity who had cele-brated his arrival in England by going on one glorious "tear," and whom Hawthorne treated to the tongue-lashing of his life and then sent back to Boston. His final opinion was that the creature "had incurred sin no further than a madman may," but this charitable judgment he veiled discreetly from the other's eyes.

Hawthorne knew his Bible well, as we have already seen in another connection.[2] "This morning my wife read to us the Sermon on the Mount, most beautifully; so that methinks even the Author of it might be satisfied with such an utterance." Many years later, as Ada Shepard reports, he was listening with the same rapture in Rome. But he did not need his wife to familiarize him with the Book of Books. There is at least one passage in *The American Magazine* where he distinguishes between it and "uninspired" literature, and when it is cast into the fire in "Earth's Holocaust" only "certain marginal notes and commentaries" are consumed. *The Pilgrim's Progress,* as we have also seen, he greatly loved and was strongly influenced by. And for all his professed dislike of theological works and his horror of the theological accumulations in the Old Manse library, we still have evidence of his having read—or at least drawn out of the library—a considerable number of theological works and religious periodicals, old and new. Moreover, he used what he read. To take but one example, he drew Jeremy

Taylor's *Ductor Dubitantium* from the Salem Athenaeum in 1834, and there is good reason to suppose that it influenced "Fancy's Show Box." [3]

Hawthorne's use of the religious ideas and conditioning which his ancestors bequeathed to him was discriminating rather than either credulous or rebellious. He did not idealize his ancestors; neither did he caricature them; and though he was sure they would have despised him as a frivolous story teller, he knew that "strong traits of their nature have intertwined themselves with mine." He did not bother to discriminate between the Pilgrims of Plymouth and the Puritans of the Massachusetts Bay Colony, and sometimes, as in "The Gray Champion," he presents the issue between his ancestors and their opponents in terms of black and white. He sympathized with Roger Williams but not with Anne Hutchinson. He weighed strength and error carefully in relation to Cotton Mather, whom he condemns in "Alice Doane's Appeal" but presents sympathetically in *Grandfather's Chair*. Endicott is an heroic figure in "Endicott and the Red Cross," and even in "The Maypole of Merry Mount" he is not without natural feeling. Hawthorne's sympathies seem to be with the Puritans in this last story, yet his Merry Mount is not a sinister or debauched place.

Puritan persecution of Quakers and witches was a special subject. Hawthorne made ambivalence a literary technique in practically all stories involving the supernatural but, in spite of his dislike of shallow "rationalism," he is perfectly clear-cut on witchcraft, as perhaps he had to be to purge himself in his own mind of the sins of his ancestors. In his stories the Salem outburst was a "terrible delusion," a "universal madness," in which "innocent persons" "died so wrongfully." [4] He is equally clear in his condemnation of Quaker persecution as such, but in his most elaborate treatment of this theme, "The

Gentle Boy," he condemns Quaker fanaticism quite as strongly as Puritan intolerance.[5]

Hawthorne was not incapable of metaphysical speculation: "I sat till eight o'clock, meditating upon this world and the next, and my dear little wife, as connected with both." Melville certainly encouraged this tendency when they were both in the Berkshires, and their very last conversation in England was heavily metaphysical. Formal theology, however, meant so little to Hawthorne that there is no general agreement on whether he was Unitarian or Trinitarian, and though he seems to think of Christ as Saviour he says little or nothing about how or why He saves.

In the religious training of his own children Hawthorne would seem to have taken his cue from Charles Lamb's "I am determined my children shall be brought up in their father's religion, if they can find out what it is."

We had always been and kept on being religious [writes Julian], but I never knew of what denomination. Unitarian seems the most likely; but what Unitarianism was I was never told, or asked, or knew, except that it was good Bostonian. . . . [My father's] reverence for the holy of holies was so profound that I never recalled hearing him speak the name of the Almighty except in reading. . . . As for the mysteries of Christ, they were never touched on; and the "One God in Three Persons" was left unchallenged. . . . I might read the Story of the Miraculous Conception and Birth in the New Testament, however, without restraint. Of course, I believed it, partly because I never heard it disputed.

Comic as this seems, it was not unnatural in the light of Hawthorne's own religious background. Even a more theologically-minded man might have had some difficulty in defining his stand. "He found his religion," writes Henry S. Kariel, "but not his theology." He never needed to revolt against his inherited Calvinism, for it had never been pressed upon him. Hawthornes had married Anglican girls as far back as the middle of the eighteenth century, and the East Salem Church, which Nathaniel attended as a boy, was described as "then on the verge of Unitarianism." Hawthorne's mother and his sister Louisa went with it into Unitarianism, but his uncle Robert Manning separated himself from it and joined an orthodox society. Both the men most likely to have influenced Hawthorne at Bowdoin—Thomas C. Upham and Dugald Stewart —had already broken with Calvinism.[6]

In "Monsieur du Miroir" as it originally appeared in 1837, "Universalist or Unitarian infidelity" was actually coupled with "Roman Church idolatry"; Hawthorne cut the sentence. when he reprinted the tale in *Mosses from an Old Manse*,[7] but which communion he was trying to spare might still be a question. On the other hand, he saved "The Celestial Railroad," and the orthodox did not misunderstand it when they reprinted it as a tract, for no more blasting indictment of those who find themselves at ease in Zion has ever been penned.

In one of his early letters Hawthorne refers to Christmas as "the holiest of holydays—the day that brought ransom to all other sinners." (He had to work.) Once in his notebooks he wondered why St. Luke did not record just what Christ told the disciples about himself when He appeared to them after his Resurrection on the occasion of their walk to Emmaus —"Whether [He was] God, or Man, or both, or something between; together with all other essential points of doctrine." In another passage he seems to take the story of the Transfiguration literally—"when the divinity and immortality of the Saviour beamed from within him through the earthly features that ordinarily shaded him." Again he wonders why Christ cursed the fig tree: "It *seems* unreasonable to have expected it to bear figs out of season." Would it not have been "as great a miracle, and far more beautiful,—and, one would think, of more beneficent influence,—to have made it suddenly rich with ripe fruit." These passages seem difficult to reconcile with a Unitarian or rationalistic conception of Christ.

II

For all his failure to commit himself in terms of a theological formulation, it is clear that the bias of Hawthorne's spirit, both in religious and in non-religious matters, was conservative and orthodox. The Catholic critic, Joseph Schwartz, conjectures that he did not affiliate because he could not go all the way with either Calvinism or Unitarianism (both, of course, heresies).[8] This is not altogether an unreasonable suggestion, and Father Fick's winning and persuasive interpretation of the religious outlook implicit in his writings [9] shows quite clearly and without ever forcing the note that Hawthorne's thinking in religious matters was at least as close to Catholicism as it was to Calvinism. In view of his refusal to accept foreordination and total depravity it was, indeed, probably much closer.

Yet Hawthorne was not a Catholic, and in spite of the fact that his conversion was rumored during his stay in Italy he was never in danger of becoming one, for this would have meant a tearing up of roots impossible for a man of his temperament. "Generally, I suspect," he says, "when people throw off the faith they were born in, the best soil of their hearts is apt to cling to its roots." He was dead long before his daughter Rose became a Catholic, but he saw Una's Anglicanism coming, and it gave him a bad moment, though, with his never-failing insistence on respecting the integrity of the individual, he at once made up his mind to accept it if it came:

Would it be well . . . for religion to be intimately connected, in her mind, with the forms and ceremonials, and sanctified places of worship? Shall the whole sky be the dome of her cathedral? —or must she compress the Deity into a narrow space, for the purpose of getting at him more readily? Wouldst thou like to have her follow Aunt Lou and Miss Rodgers into the musty old Church of England? This looks very probable to me; but thou wilt know best how it is, and likewise whether it had better be so, or not. If it is natural for Una to remain within these tenets, she will be happiest there; but if her moral and intellectual development should compel her hereafter to break from them, it would be with the more painful wrench for once having accepted them.

Hawthorne's exposure to Catholicism came largely in Rome; I find no indication of his having read any Catholic books beyond the classics which all Christendom reads. He said many things about the Church which Catholics must find painful reading, as in his references to "the old, corrupted faith of Rome" and the "torpid recluses" shut up in monasteries and nunneries. But the surprising thing about Hawthorne in Rome is not what he missed but what he saw. What really distressed him was that the lives of Italian priests and laymen failed to measure up to the glory of the faith they professed, and that is not an anti-Catholic point of view at all. It is interesting to note that though he had wavered in his judgment of Cotton Mather on other scores, he had always condemned him for his "hard-hearted, pedantic" bigotry toward Catholics. At no time in his life was there any doubt in his mind concerning the imperative need of religious toleration. "American statesmanship comprises Jew, Catholic, all." His campaign biography of Franklin Pierce praises him specifically for his stand against anti-Catholic discrimination. Hawthorne liked the atmosphere of prayer in Rome. He liked the devotional spirit he saw all about him. He understood and appreciated the marvelous adaptation of the Catholic faith to human need. For a New England Protestant he was amazingly understanding about indulgences. His classification of sins was basically in harmony with that of Aquinas. Above all, he appreciated the spiritual and therapeutic values of the confessional. It is true that Charlotte Brontë's

Lucy Snowe had stormed the confessional for her need before Hawthorne's Hilda, but Professor Fairbanks is surely right when he finds Charlotte Brontë condescending compared to Hawthorne. Nor had Hawthorne waited until he got to Rome to conceive this idea. He had once considered the daring device of having Dimmesdale confess his sin to a priest, and perhaps it was only the difficulty of fitting such a situation into a seventeenth-century Boston milieu that caused him to give up the idea.[10]

III

Catholicism was not the only faith foreign to Hawthorne's background which made a bid for his attention. For he lived in an age when spiritualism and other forms of occultism were attracting many—"the mysticism, or, rather, the mystic sensuality of this secular age," as he calls it in *The Blithedale Romance*. Miss Hosmer has plausibly suggested that he may first have heard of spiritualism when he visited the Shakers at Canterbury, New Hampshire, in 1831; in any event his interest antedated the career of the Fox sisters. When his cousin Lucy Sutton came to play with him as a child in Salem, he would take her to play in the old carriage and livery stable, telling her that "all the people who used to ride in them were dead, and now their ghosts came and peeped out at him." Later he asked her whether she had seen a witch in passing Gallows Hill. Apparently he and Bridge often consulted a fortune teller at Bowdoin: "I never refuse to take a glimpse into futurity," says the narrator of "The Seven Vagabonds." According to Symmes there were many ghost stories in Hawthorne's disputed Raymond diary. There are only two in the part that has been printed, one of which concludes with the charmingly characteristic observation, "I should not be willing to sleep in that garret, though I do not believe a word of the story."

Hawthorne reviewed Whittier's *The Supernaturalism of New England* very severely on the ground that the author was too condescending toward his materials. "If he cannot believe his ghost-story while he is telling it, he had better leave the task to somebody else."

Temperamentally too Hawthorne was strongly anti-materialist. Few men can ever have had a stronger "strangers and pilgrims" feeling in the world. "The grosser life is a dream," he told Sophia, "and the spiritual life a reality." He never anywhere felt "more permanently located than the traveller who sits down to rest by the road which he is plodding along." [11]

Hawthorne had independent psychic experiences also. I am not referring now to the vague "we have been here before" feeling which he refers to in both "The Ancestral Footstep" and *Dr. Grimshawe's Secret*, nor yet to the attempts he and Sophia made to practice what we should now call "extra-sensory perception." [12] He himself has described [13] how he saw the ghost of old Dr. Harris not once but many times in his accustomed place at the Boston Athenaeum. We do not need to cite Hawthorne's complete trustworthiness in all matters of testimony to be sure that he really had this experience; no creative writer could possibly "make up" such a dull, flat ghost story as he has given us. "I have no recollection of being greatly discomposed at the moment, nor indeed that I felt any extraordinary emotion whatever." "I might have tested him in a hundred ways; but I did nothing of the kind." This is not the way people behave in fiction when they see a ghost. But it is the way they behave in life, as anybody who has ever had such an experience can testify. Shortly before his marriage Hawthorne reported to Sophia that he had not seen Dr. Harris lately:

Foolish me, not to have accosted him; for perhaps he wished to give us some good advice on our entrance into connubial life—or possibly, he intended to disclose the hiding-place of some ancient hoard of gold, which would have freed us forever from all pecuniary cares. I think we shall not need his counsel on the former point; but on the latter, it would have been peculiarly acceptable.

Dr. Harris was no unique phenomenon, for two of the houses Hawthorne inhabited were haunted—the Old Manse and the Mall Street house in Salem, where he lived while he was employed in the custom house.

At the Manse:

Our ghost used to heave deep sighs in a particular corner of the parlor, and sometimes rustled paper, as if he were turning over a sermon in the long upper entry,—where nevertheless he was invisible in spite of the bright moonshine that fell in through the eastern window. Not improbably he wished me to edit and publish a selection from a chest full of manuscript discourses that stood in the garret. Once, while Hillard and other friends sat talking with us in the twilight, there came a rustling noise as of a minister's silk gown, sweeping through the very midst of the company so closely as almost to brush against the chairs. Still there was nothing visible. A yet stranger business was that of a ghostly servant maid, who used to be heard in the kitchen at deepest midnight, grinding coffee, cooking, ironing,—performing, in short, all kinds of domestic labor, —although no traces of anything accomplished could be detected the next morning. Some neglected duty of her servitude—some ill-starched ministerial band—disturbed the poor damsel in her grave and kept her at work without any wages.

And at Mall Street:

An apparition haunts our front-yard. I have often, while sitting in the parlor, in the day-time, had a perception that somebody was passing the windows—but, on looking towards them, nobody is there. The appearance is never observable when looking directly towards the window, but only by such a side-long or indirect glance as one gets while reading, or intent on something else. But I know not how many times I have raised my head, or turned towards the window, with a certainty that somebody was passing. The other day, I found that my wife was equally aware of this spectre, and that—as likewise agrees with my own observation—it always appears to be entering the yard from the street, never going out.

I have found no indication that Hawthorne ever attended any spiritualist séances in America, but he did in Florence, where he and Sophia were drawn into the Browning circle, and where their own governess Ada Shepard, herself unwilling and unbelieving, manifested a flair for automatic writing.[14] According to Miss Shepard there were "fierce arguments" at the Hawthorne board every day, with Hawthorne "very logically and very severely" tearing Mrs. Hawthorne's "strongholds" to pieces.

Why, then, was Hawthorne so hostile to spiritualism? He does not attempt to controvert the testimony in its favor. He says frankly that on any other subject he would accept such testimony without question. Intellectually, though not emotionally, he can even be called open-minded. In his talks with the sculptor Hiram Powers, who was a believer, he even suggested the possibility that the human race may share the earth with other beings "of whose existence and whereabout we could have no perception, nor they of ours, because we are endowed with different sets of senses." But, as Miss Hosmer remarks, even when his reason was convinced, his intuition balked, and Hawthorne always had less respect for his reason than for his intuition.

It is clear that the phenomena of the séance room are as repugnant to some natures as they are fascinating to others; Hawthorne was in the first class. He felt "a sluggish disgust, and a repugnance to meddle with it." No doubt it would have been easier for him if the messages that came through had been less puerile, if through them something had been communicated which was too lofty for merely human wisdom. The contrary seemed to him to be the case, and that to such an extent that

if the messages in question really did emanate from their puta-
tive sources, he could only suppose the "spirits" involved to
have become almost imbecilic since passing over to the other
side.

To hold intercourse with spirits of this order, we must stoop and
grovel in some element more vile than earthly dust. These goblins,
if they exist at all, are but the shadows of past mortality, outcasts,
mere refuse stuff, adjudged unworthy of the eternal world, and, on
the most favorable supposition, dwindling gradually into nothing-
ness.

But even this was not Hawthorne's root objection. He did
not believe spiritistic communications to have any religious
meaning or significance, and he quotes Christ's saying that
unbelievers would not change their minds "though one rose
from the dead." The authentication of spiritual matters by
material means seemed monstrous to him—"the view which I
take upon this matter is caused by no want of faith in mysteries,
but from a deep reverence of the soul and the mysteries which
it knows within itself, but never transmits to the earthly eye
and ear"—and he shuddered over the possibilities of confusing
the two.

Without distrusting that the phenomena have really occurred,
I think that they are to be accounted for as the result of a material
and physical, not of a spiritual, influence. Opium has produced
many a brighter vision of heaven, I fancy, and just as susceptible
of proof, as these. . . . And what delusion can be more lamentable
and mischievous, than to mistake the physical and material for the
spiritual? What so miserable as to lose the soul's true, though
hidden, knowledge and consciousness of heaven in the mist of an
earth-born vision? [15]

Hawthorne's attitude toward other borderline psychic and
religious movements resembled his attitude toward spiritualism.

He perceived their kinship to ancient necromancy, and theoretically he was willing to grant the possibility that "modern psychology" might ultimately "reduce" them "to a system." Practically he wanted nothing to do with them. Mesmerism plays a considerable role in *The House of the Seven Gables* and *The Blithedale Romance*, but Hawthorne treated it even more unsympathetically than he treated spiritualism, for it seemed to him to open up a way for one human being to invade or secure control of the psychic being of another.

He may have seen or heard of Anna Q. T. Parsons, a gifted psychometrist in whom the Brook Farm people were interested, and there is an interesting reference to psychometry in "A Book of Autographs." On phrenology he reaches no conclusion. I have found nothing on numerology beyond the fact that Una as a child once asked him, for no particular reason, to write the number "64" on her hand; he did so, and thereafter continued to write "64" whenever he "doodled"— "probably there is some destiny connected with this particular number," he says. There was, for he died in 1864. He also once attended at Sanborn's house in Concord an exposition of a new method of medical or psycho-medical treatment in which his sister-in-law Mrs. Mann was interested and from which, it was thought, Una might benefit.

IV

Hawthorne once tenderly reassured a little girl who came to him in tears because she had been told he was an infidel. More sophisticated persons have often made the same mistake. In spite of all Hawthorne's uncertainties, what he believed was large and important. He believed in God. He believed in immortality. He believed in Divine Providence. He believed in the infinite value of every human soul.

About the first of these beliefs he says nothing whatever in an argumentative way, for the excellent reason that it never occurred to him that there was anything to argue about. He could no more have doubted God than he could have doubted life itself. He could be flippant, as when he wrote, "I thank God (whenever I happen to think of it)," for, like Dickens, he loathed cant, and he knew that those who have God constantly upon their lips often have the least of Him in their hearts. But he could be simply and sincerely earnest too, as when, in his youth, he was shocked and repelled by the "damnably perverted" religious notions of the Frenchman Schaeffer. He habitually thought of God as the giver of every good and perfect gift and as the only refuge of otherwise helpless men. "Pray GOD for it, my Dove," he tells Sophia—"for you know how to pray better than I do." And again, about one of her pictures, "Thou couldst not have done it, unless God had helped thee." He did not think of the age in which he lived as a great age of prayer but he was sure that Hepzibah's prayer was heard in heaven, and he made Coverdale think better of Hollingsworth because he prayed. When Una seemed to have recovered from her illness he gave the credit to "God's providence and a good constitution" and not to medicine. Best of all, there is Bliss Perry's beautiful story of the time Hawthorne sent a sunflower to his sorrowing neighbors with the message, "Tell them that the sunflower is a symbol of the sun, and that the sun is a symbol of the glory of God." [16]

About immortality he says more. Yet he does not give the impression of being obsessed by the subject. Once William Allingham told him Tennyson had said that "if he were sure there were no hereafter, he would go and fling himself over London Bridge;—a foolish thing," adds Hawthorne, "to do or to say." With him there was no struggle, only a calm assurance.

Contact with death strains faith for many men, but when Hawthorne stood beside his mother's death bed he exclaimed,

Oh what a mockery, if what I saw were all,—let the interval between extreme youth and dying age be filled up with what happiness it might! But God would not have made the close so dark and wretched, if there were nothing beyond; for then it would have been a fiend that created us, and measured out our existence, and not God. It would be something beyond wrong—it would be insult —to be thrust out of life into annihilation in this miserable way. So, out of the very bitterness of death, I gather the sweet assurance of a better state of being.

He was pleased when Leigh Hunt affirmed his hope of immortality, and felt closer drawn to him in consequence, and he was shocked and grieved when Harriet Martineau denied it. "I will not think so, were it only for her sake;—only a few weeds to spring out of her fat mortality, instead of her intellect and sympathies flowering and fruiting forever." In his writings for children he hopes that Anne Hutchinson's Indian-reared daughter was reunited with her mother in heaven and thinks of Sir Isaac Newton as carrying on his work in the spiritual world. He promised Bridge that he would regain in Eternity the daughter he had lost here, and he sweetens what would otherwise be the cynical end of "The Wedding Knell" by presenting it as "the union of two immortal souls." Even a beautiful day is "the promise of a blissful eternity." Man needed immortality not only to compensate him for his misery here—on that score justice demands extending it even to animals—but as a means of realizing his full human possibilities.

Sometimes he turns from faith to speculation, as when he sees the dying melting "into the great multitude of the Departed as quietly as a drop of water into the ocean," so that perhaps they are "conscious of no unfamiliarity with their circumstances, but immediately become aware of an insufferable strangeness in the world which they have quitted. Death has not taken them away but brought them home." Thus he attempted to comfort Sophia over her brother's death during their courtship: "He is already at home in the Celestial city, more at home than ever he was in his mother's house." I find only one suggestion of life weariness. Hawthorne is reported to have told Edward Dicey that he hoped there would be a break between this life and the next: "A couple of thousand years or so of sleep is the least that I can do with before I begin life again."

He loathed the whole hideous nineteenth-century ritual of funerals and graveyards—"our thoughts should follow the celestial soul and not the earthly corpse"—and in *American Magazine* days he was shocked by the announced discovery of a method for turning human bodies to stone and preserving them forever:

> In God's own time, we would fain be buried as our fathers were. We desire to give mortality its own. Our clay must not be baulked of its repose. . . . We have no yearnings for the grossness of this earthly immortality. If somewhat of our soul and intellect might live in the memory of men, we should be glad. . . . But what belongs to the earth, let the earth take it.

As all readers of *Septimius Felton* know, Hawthorne thought a good deal about earthly immortality. The death of Washington Allston before he had finished *Belshazzar's Feast* caused him to speculate—*Back to Methuselah*-fashion—on what it would mean to be able to be sure of life until our work were done. But though he wavers somewhat in his attitude, he knows that life as we live it here gains in charm and value through its transitoriness, and that for the man who should attain it, abnormally long life would be a barrier between himself and his fellows or even, as it was for the Wandering Jew, a burden. There are a number of interesting passages in which Hawthorne almost seems to commit himself to the traditional Christian and medieval idea that the man who is well-adjusted to this world is sure to be maladjusted to Eternity. Man being a spiritual being, it was not God's will that he should find all he needed here. Septimius Felton sins in a very different way from Aylmer of "The Birthmark" but they both sin, and both are condemned for seeking in time what can only exist outside of it.

As a man with a Calvinistic inheritance, Hawthorne had to do more thinking about Providence than about immortality. The old Calvinistic foreordination and election were not for him, and depravity in his eyes was universal but not total; "fate endowed with sympathy," he tells Sophia, "becomes not a fate but a Providence." Sometimes his application of this faith to specific situations may seem a little naïve. "I trust that God means to put me in some other position," he writes. And again, of Una, "If Providence had not done it, as thou sayest, I should deeply regret her having been present at this recent grief-time of the O'Sullivans." Yet he was not ignorant of the philosophical problems involved in reconciling free will and destiny. He recognized the limitations imposed on freedom of choice by inheritance and temperament and, above all, by our own acts, which may, at last, so enmesh us that the area in which we are able to move freely is very narrow. But even for Dimmesdale, an enmeshed man if ever there was one, the possibility of saving action remains to the end.[17]

For Hawthorne Providence was a loving Providence, because God was a loving God. During his early days a young man was drowned in Crooked River. The Freewill Baptist minister who preached his funeral sermon was doubtful of his salvation, but if the Symmes diary be genuine, Hawthorne did not share this view. "I read one of the Psalms to my mother, and it plainly declares twenty-six times, that 'God's mercy endureth forever.' " He strikes exactly the same note when he rejects Michelangelo's Jesus in his picture of the Last Judgment as

not looking in the least like the Saviour of the world, but with uplifted arm, denouncing eternal misery on those whom he came to save. I fear I am myself among the wicked, for I found myself inevitably taking their part, and asking for at least a little pity, some few regrets, and not such a stern denunciatory spirit on the part of Him who had thought us worth dying for.

As for the value of those souls, not even Cardinal Newman, who believed that it would be better for the world to be destroyed than for one soul to sin, was more convinced of it than Hawthorne. In life it shows best in his touching descriptions of outcast English children:

It might almost make a man doubt the existence of his own soul, to observe how Nature [note that he does not say "God," for he cannot connect the thought of God with such outrage] has flung these little wretches into the street and left them there, so evidently regarding them as nothing worth, and how all mankind acquiesce in the great mother's estimate of her offspring. For, if they are to have no immortality, what superior claim can I assert for mine? And how difficult to believe that anything so precious as a germ of immortal growth can have been buried under this dirt-heap, plunged into this cesspool of misery and vice! . . . The whole question of eternity is staked there. If a single one of those helpless little ones be lost, the world is lost!

He goes on to tell the story of the terrible scrofulous workhouse child who attached itself to him, expecting to be taken up and fondled and whom he accommodated in expiation of his brother's blood guilt. Only we must go to *The English Notebooks* to learn that Hawthorne was himself the child's victim; in *Our Old Home* he changes himself to "one member of our party" and "a person burdened with more than an Englishman's customary reserve." "It was as if God had promised the child this favor on my behalf," he told his notebook, "and that I must needs fulfil the contract. . . . I should never have forgiven myself if I had repelled its advances."

Long before he had written in his *American Notebooks:*

The Unpardonable Sin might consist in a want of love and reverence for the Human Soul; in consequence of which, the investigator pried into its dark depths, not with a hope or purpose of making it better, but from a cold philosophical curiosity,—content that it should be wicked in whatever kind or degree, and only desiring to study it out. Would not this, in other words, be the separation of the intellect from the heart? [18]

It was a sin to which the artist was particularly liable, as Hawthorne well knew, and from which he could save himself only by remembering something like what Shorthouse has said in *John Ingelsant,* that "Nothing less than Infinite pity is sufficient for the Infinite pathos of human life." Dimmesdale is a sinner, but he is right when he cries to Hester in the forest: "We are not, Hester, the worst sinners in the world. There is one worse than even the polluted priest! That old man's revenge has been blacker than my sin. He has violated in cold blood, the sanctity of a human heart. Thou and I, Hester, never did so!"

Rappaccini and Ethan Brand are lost because they use human beings as things; Aylmer, confusing, as Melville might put it, horological and chronometrical time, sacrifices his wife to his own mad dream of an impossible, earthly, material perfection. In Hawthorne's morality, as in that of Henry James, damnation may even be incurred by establishing control over another's soul for benevolent purposes, since it is impious to put oneself into the place of God. Or, rather, to put one's self into a place which even God would not think it fitting to occupy, since Milton had taught Hawthorne that God allowed Adam and

Eve to sin themselves out of Eden, because, if they were not free to choose, goodness could have no more meaning for them than evil. It is astonishing how many of Hawthorne's greatest "villains" were led to their doom by noble motives. Who ever aimed higher than Ethan Brand? And even Chillingworth devoted his life to the relief of suffering and began his study of Dimmesdale himself "desirous only of truth." In a sense, then, Hawthorne seems to have believed that it is every man's right to go to hell if he wants to, or at least that no other man has the moral right to use force to prevent him.

V

Like Henry James again, Hawthorne had a very keen sense of the presence of evil in the world. But he was not obsessed with it. Young Goodman Brown was obsessed by it and he wasted his life. Roderick Ellison was obsessed by it until his purging, and his only interest in life was to find others with serpents in their bosoms to match his own. Pride is a disease, and the monstrousness of human egotism is such that an Ellison or an Ethan Brand may cherish even affliction and monstrous malformation because it sets him apart from others, destroys the sense of fellowship which gives others a claim upon him, and bolsters his conceit of himself. Hawthorne views evil from the point of view of a man who is himself committed to virtue; the "raptures and roses of vice" are not for him. This is not because he does not understand them. On the contrary, he does understand them, understands them as only a man can who is detached from them and has a perspective on them. Miriam and Donatello find "rapture," "nobility," and "an ecstatic sense of freedom" through the guilt they share, but they also think of themselves as united with all sinners and estranged from all saints,[19] and even Hester tells Dimmesdale in the forest that "what we did had a consecration of its own."

Hawthorne was sufficiently sensitive to feel that one may incur guilt in dreams, or that the soul may stain itself by thinking sin without actually committing it. But he was also sane enough to know that there is a difference between planning a murder and carrying out the plan.

Roy R. Male makes an acute suggestion when he remarks that by putting the sin of Hester and Dimmesdale into the antecedent action of *The Scarlet Letter* Hawthorne made it a type of original sin. But though he secured this effect he may not have intended it, and we may be sure that he would have handled the situation as he did whether or no. One can hardly think of him as tracing the process of the seduction. In *The Marble Faun* he never explains Miriam's antecedent mystery and seems determined to suggest both that she is guilty and that she is innocent. Sometimes he doubted the social utility of the literature of crime. In *Peter Parley's Universal History* he even worried about whether children might not be contaminated by the evil deeds they must necessarily read about in history. Many authors find it much easier to describe evil characters than good ones. This was not true of Hawthorne, whose "villains," as we have seen, are likely to suggest a literary origin. When he looked in his heart to write he did not find evil there.

Yet Hawthorne was never guilty of over-simplification in his presentation of evil—nor of good either. God gave Hester "a lovely child" as the "direct consequence" of the sin which man punished by fastening a scarlet letter on her bosom, and indeed the letter itself comes, during its wearer's life of service, to take on "the effect of the cross on a nun's bosom. It imparted to the wearer a kind of sacredness, which enabled her to walk securely amid all peril." Yet neither here nor in *The Marble Faun*, where both Miriam and Kenyon speculate dar-

ingly on the way in which good can come out of evil, does
Hawthorne really commit himself to an antinomian position.

"Sin has educated Donatello, and elevated him. Is sin, then,—which
we deem such a dreadful blackness in the universe,—is it, like
sorrow, merely an element of human education, through which we
struggle to a higher and purer state than we could otherwise have
attained? Did Adam fall, that we might ultimately rise to a far
loftier paradise than his?"

According to Dorothy Waples [20] and others, the real subject
of *The Marble Faun* is "nature improved by a share of guilt,"
but Hawthorne "tempers it to the shorn lambs who may read
it." This, I fear, is to show no more knowledge of the background of Christian thinking on the subject of the "fortunate
fall" than John Erskine did when, many years ago, he sought
to impute similar heresies to Milton and was annihilated by
E. E. Stoll, Sir Herbert Grierson, Arthur O. Lovejoy, and
others. *"O felix culpa quae talem et tantum meruit habere
redemptorem"*—thus reads the passage in the Exultet for the
Holy Saturday Mass. Professor Stewart has recently quoted [21]
Adam's ponderings from the last book of *Paradise Lost:*

> Full of doubt I stand
> Whether I should repent me now of sin
> By me done and occasioned, or rejoice
> Much more that much more good thereof shall spring
> To God more glory, more good-will to men
> From God—and over wrath grace shall abound.

But Professor Stewart is much too intelligent to stop there:

St. Paul has raised the same question. "Shall we continue in sin,"
he asks, "that grace may abound?" And answers, "God forbid."
But he had previously said that "where sin abounded, grace did
much more abound."

Hawthorne never proclaims salvation through sin. He goes
much farther than most Christian moralists have gone in pro-

claiming the sinfulness of sin. "And be the stern and sad truth spoken, that the breach which guilt has once made into the human soul is never, in this mortal state, repaired." Even misfortunes like Clifford Pyncheon's, which are not the result of sin, cannot be made up for. "After such wrong as he had suffered," says Hawthorne, "there is no reparation." And how scornful Holgrave is toward Hollingsworth's plan to reform criminals by appealing to their higher instincts. "He ought to have commenced his investigation by perpetrating some huge sin in his own proper person, and examining the condition of his higher instincts afterwards."

Any obscurities which may appear in Hawthorne's attitude on this matter are due to his realism, his understanding of ethical complexities, and his determination to present the problem on a higher level than one adapted to the primary class. Go back for a moment to the drunken clergyman in Liverpool:

I leave it to members of his own profession to decide whether it was better for him thus to sin outright, and so be let into the miserable secret of what manner of man he was, or to have gone through life outwardly unspotted, making the first discovery of his latent evil at the judgment-seat. It has occurred to me that this dire calamity, as both he and I regarded it, may have been the only method by which precisely such a man as himself . . . could be redeemed.

"*Could* be redeemed"—not *will* be redeemed. Hawthorne was a man, not a child, and he knew that he lived—as we do —in a fallen world. To that extent sin is inevitable, and the man who claims to be free of it is the worst sinner of all and the one whom all healthy sinners must avoid like the plague. But sin is not therefore less lethal. As the condition of our prisons and mental hospitals eloquently testifies, it does not lose its effect if you stop describing it in theological language and use instead the latest psychological lingo. "When poisons become fashionable," says C. S. Lewis, "they do not cease to kill." Redemption can only come through repentance and amendment of life, and if these are absent it will not come at all.

Nor will it do to reply to this that Hester does not repent but is nevertheless admirable. Of course Hester is admirable, humanly speaking, but she does not solve her spiritual problem without repentance.[22] And of course grace cannot abound where sin has not abounded; it is only the White Queen who summons a physician to cure an illness which has not yet occurred. But this does not mean that sin is grace nor sickness health. There is no Swinburnian swooning in Shakespeare's "soul of goodness in things evil"; there is only a recognition of the fact that nothing that God has made can be utterly corrupted. And to see men redeemed through the suffering and sorrow which may follow sin is not to ascribe to sin itself a starry-eyed healing virtue; it is simply to accept thankfully the operations of Divine Grace under the only conditions in which any of us can expect to encounter them while we are in this life. What Mary E. Coleridge so well wrote about Hawthorne's attitude on this matter in 1904 has been abundantly confirmed by all well-advised study since that time:

Capricious as he felt the world to be, he never speculated as to the Power that made it, as the end for which it was made, as to the wickedness of everything that runs counter to that end. The world was made by "Providence"; it was made for the expansion and improvement of man; it was marred by sin, and sin is excessively sinful and never can be anything else.[23]

VI

Hawthorne's personality has often been regarded as enigmatic. Every man's heart is an unfathomable mystery—even sometimes to himself. But this was not notably truer of Hawthorne than of other men. Of late there has been a certain tendency to make a mystery even of his dying, and "What was wrong with Hawthorne?" has become one of the teasing questions of American literary biography.

We hear of deafness, chills, indigestion, loss of vigor and of weight, assorted aches and pains, and one terrible attack of nose-bleeding which lasted for twenty-four hours. Anyone who has compared his penmanship during the last years with what he had previously produced will find it difficult to avoid feeling that Hawthorne had suddenly become a very old man. Hawthorne "looks gray and grand," wrote Longfellow in 1863, "with something very pathetic about him." And when, in April 1864, he returned to Concord from Philadelphia, where he had seen Ticknor die, Mrs. Hawthorne was "frightened out of all knowledge" of herself by the sight of his face "so haggard, so white, so deeply scored with pain and fatigue."

Except for Oliver Wendell Holmes's report of his last talk with Hawthorne, we have, by way of diagnosis, only the guesses of Mrs. Hawthorne and Fields, and Franklin Pierce's conjecture that his brain and/or spine must have been affected at the end because he walked and used his hands with difficulty. That his mind might go was the hideous fear that had plagued Hawthorne himself, and when Mrs. Hawthorne heard that Holmes had suggested this, she was almost beside herself: her penciled scrawl to Fields about it, utterly unlike her usual handwriting, still affects the reader as a moving cry of distress. Of course even Holmes had no opportunity to make a proper examination of Hawthorne. He had "refused all along to see a doctor," but when Sophia "discovered that it is only to a homeopathic physician he has an objection," Una at once got a letter off to Mrs. Fields asking her to arrange to have Holmes encounter him "accidentally on purpose," as the saying is. The Peabodys were all passionate homeopaths, and when Mrs.

Hawthorne and the children were ill, they were treated by homeopaths, though once, in London, in 1856, Hawthorne did call in an allopath for his wife, being "inclined to put faith in what is tangible." Yet he had been so horrified by the allopathic treatments to which he saw Ticknor subjected in Philadelphia that his special antipathy to homeopathy at this particular time is not without its surprising aspects.

Dr. Holmes found "nothing . . . that gave warning of so sudden an end" as soon appeared, but he could not regard Hawthorne's general "aspect" as other than "very unfavorable."

There were persistent local symptoms, referred especially to the stomach,—"boring pain," distension, difficult digestion, with great wasting of flesh and strength. He was very gentle, very willing to answer questions, very docile to such counsel as I offered him, but evidently had no hope of recovering his health. He spoke as if his work were done, and he should write no more.

A psychologically (or pseudo-psychologically) oriented age is not, however, content to leave it there. We have long been accustomed to critics who have tied up Hawthorne's physical breakdown with his unhappiness about the Civil War and the failure of his powers as a writer as manifested in his inability to complete either *Septimius Felton* or *Dr. Grimshawe's Secret*. Both these factors must have exercised a depressing effect. Even Jane Addams, whose estrangement from World War I was certainly far more firmly grounded ideationally and philosophically than Hawthorne's from the Civil War, afterwards testified that she sometimes "secretly yearned to participate in the folly of all mankind." And what could possibly have a more depressing effect on a writer's health than the fear that his power had failed him?

Recently, however, in what is surely the most determined effort that has yet been made to probe Hawthorne's psyche at the close of his life, Hyatt H. Waggoner [24] has seen fit to bring a hypothetical Oedipus complex into the picture, along with "lifelong restlessness, unease, and sense of guilt or estrangement." One cannot but admire Professor Waggoner's courage in grappling with a very difficult problem, but perhaps one might be inclined to respect his findings more if they did not quite so slavishly adhere to the conventional Freudian pattern. If one could devise a Freudian Univac to diagnose the "case" of writers long dead and "unanalyzed" during their lifetime, and feed it the kind of materials Professor Waggoner has been fed, it might safely be trusted to come up with his results. There is simply no evidence that during his later years Hawthorne lost his faith in immortality or any of the other anchors with which his ship had been equipped since childhood, while as for the "typical liberal views" of the period, which Professor Waggoner sees him as having finally relinquished, the only thing that needs to be said is that he had never entertained them. In his last conversation with Melville it was not faith and immortality that Hawthorne found "dismal" subjects, as Professor Waggoner seems to think; it was merely Melville's life- and energy-paralyzing attitude toward them.

Moreover, there is a great deal in Hawthorne's behavior toward the close of his life to refute the notion that he had lost the will to live to any greater extent than one would expect of a man who was physically as sick as he was. "He never seemed old to us . . ." writes Julian, "even to the last. There was a primitive freshness in him, that was always arching his eyebrow and twisting the corners of his mouth." He continued to dress for dinner. He kept at his work, passionately desiring to produce one more important work, perhaps his greatest. He seized upon every favorable symptom as marking the turning of the tide back towards health.

In January 1861 he wrote a friend that he did not consider himself an old man yet. In November he was writing Fields that *Septimius* would be "a pretty long story" and wondering whether Smith and Elder would want it for the *Cornhill* and whether he ought to go to London to secure copyright there. In April 1862 he wrote Sophia from Washington that his trip had done him great good "but being perfectly well, I no longer need it as a medicine."

Even in the year he died he did not give up hope. To the old man in "The Dolliver Romance" Hawthorne attributed an inability to believe health gone forever or himself grown old. Bernard Cohen, I think, is fully justified when he complains that critics have been so busy with the aesthetic shortcomings of *Septimius Felton* that they have forgotten its philosophical content, which is sound and sane and deeply Christian. "If Hawthorne had been able to fuse form and content in the same way that he had done in *The Scarlet Letter*, *Septimius Felton* might have been ranked as his greatest novel."

We do not know why Hawthorne's health broke down as it did at the beginning of the 'sixties. We do not know whether the causes were wholly physical or whether a psychosomatic factor was involved, and it is unlikely that we shall ever find out. Unless and until we do, we shall gain nothing by being either fanciful or melodramatic about it.

Nathaniel Hawthorne had his limitations as an artist and as a man. His range as a writer was more deep than wide; there were aspects of experience that did not interest him very much; he often said no where most men say yes. Of course he was conscious of his shortcomings at times; he was a man, not an animal. We know more about the dark places of the heart of man—and about the tigerish aspects of the world—today than we did fifty years ago, but nothing that we have learned makes him seem a lesser writer than he seemed then. Even his suspicion of scientists, once set down to mere obscurantism, seems to men facing the danger of destruction by atomic energy considerably less unreasonable than it once did.

He could be stubborn and wilful, for he was a human being. He was sensitive and highly cultivated, with a streak of human coarseness occasionally showing through all his spirituality. He was kind and loving, but he was sometimes cold and kind at the same time. There was a dark side to him, but he faced the light. If there was a potential Ethan Brand in him or a young Goodman Brown, he watched him and guarded against him and strangled him. In the end darkness encompassed the weakness of his body and dragged him down, but his soul passed into the light which derives from God and illuminates the whole exhilarating, infinitely varied realm of world art.

NOTES

For the purpose of this section, see p. 221.

Both here and in the bibliographical note which follows the following abbreviations are employed:

ABC	American Book Company	LSUP	Louisiana State University Press
AL	*American Literature*	M	The Macmillan Company
BUSE	*Boston University Studies in English*	*MLN*	*Modern Language Notes*
CE	*College English*	*NCF*	*Nineteenth Century Fiction*
EIHC	*Essex Institute Historical Collections*	*NEQ*	*New England Quarterly*
		NQ	*Notes and Queries*
Fla	University of Florida Press	Okla	University of Oklahoma Press
H	Harper & Brothers		
HB	Harcourt, Brace and Company	*PMLA*	*Publications of the Modern Language Association*
HM	Houghton Mifflin Company	*PQ*	*Philological Quarterly*
HUP	Harvard University Press	*UKCR*	*University of Kansas City Review*
LB	Little, Brown and Company	*UTSE*	*University of Texas Studies in English*
LG	Longmans, Green and Company	YUP	Yale University Press

CHAPTER ONE: A MAN OF OLD SALEM

1 The fullest account of the family is in Vernon Loggins's excellent book, *The Hawthornes* (Columbia University Press, 1951).

2 Only Edward H. Davidson's edition of *Dr. Grimshawe's Secret* (HUP, 1954), gives us the text as Hawthorne left it; for Davidson's discussion of *Septimius Felton* et al., see his *Hawthorne's Last Phase* (YUP, 1949).

3   All that is known about this is recorded in two articles by Randall Stewart: "Mrs. Hawthorne's Quarrel with James T. Fields," *More Books*, XXI (1946), 254-63, and "'Pestifeous Gail Hamilton,' James T. Fields, and the Hawthornes," *NEQ*, XVII (1944), 418-23. Whatever the rights and wrongs of the matter, affairs had been conducted in a woefully unsystematic fashion for which the publishers, as experienced businessmen, were much more to blame than the innocent Hawthornes.

4   Known in her later years as Mother Alphonsa, O.S.D., Rose Hawthorne Lathrop was technically "a Dominican of the Third Order, with special permission to wear the habit and live in a community of religious." See Henry G. Fairbanks, "Hawthorne and the Catholic Church," *BUSE*, I (1955), 148-65. Her story has been told by Katherine Burton, *Sorrow Built a Bridge* (LG, 1938) and by Theodore Maynard, *A Fire Was Lighted* (Bruce, 1948). For a brief account of the later lives of all the Hawthorne children, see Loggins, op. cit.

5   "Poe, Hawthorne, and Melville: An Essay in Sociological Criticism," *Partisan Review*, XVI (1949), 157-65.

6   "Nathaniel Hawthorne's Blue Cloak," *Bookman* (New York), LXXV (1932), 501-6.

7   This idea is well expounded by Chester E. Eisinger, "Hawthorne as Champion of the Middle Way," *NEQ*, XXVII (1954), 27-52.

8   For the facts and opinions that have been recorded in this somewhat complicated matter, see R. F. Metzdorf, "Hawthorne's Suit Against Ripley and Dana," *AL*, XII (1940), 235-41; cf. Laurence S. Hall, *Hawthorne, Critic of Society* (YUP, 1944), pp. 4-5.

9   Op. cit., pp. 51ff.

Chapter Two: LEARNING AND DOING

1   The best study of this matter is in Elizabeth Ruth Hosmer's unpublished Ph.D. dissertation, "Science and Pseudo-Science in the Writings of Nathaniel Hawthorne," University of Illinois, 1948. See also Roy R. Male, "Hawthorne and the Concept of Sympathy," *PMLA*, LXVIII (1953), 138-49, and Marvin Laser, "'Head,'

'Heart,' and 'Will' in Hawthorne's Psychology," *NCF*, X (1955), 130-40.

2 Hawthorne hardly knew enough about technology to take up an attitude toward it, but see Henry G. Fairbanks, "Hawthorne and the Machine Age," *AL*, XXVIII (1956), 155-63.

3 For further comment on Hawthorne's reading, see Julian Hawthorne, *Hawthorne Reading* (Cleveland, The Rowfant Club, 1902); Austin Warren's introduction to his *Nathaniel Hawthorne: Representative Selections* (ABC, 1934); M. L. Kesselring, "Hawthorne's Reading," *Bulletin New York Public Library*, LIII (1949), 55-71, 121-38, 173-94.

4 Making due allowance for his enthusiastic family's partiality—Julian thought him better than Dickens and Mrs. Hawthorne preferred his reading to "any acting or opera"—it still seems clear that Hawthorne must have been a very gifted reader. See Rose Hawthorne Lathrop, *Works*, "Old Manse Edition," I, xxiv-xxv. For Hawthorne's use of Spenser see Randall Stewart, "Hawthorne and *The Faerie Queene*," *PQ*, XII (1933), 196-206; Hazel T. Emry, "Two Houses of Pride: Spenser's and Hawthorne's," *PQ*, XXXIII (1954), 91-4; Herbert A. Leibowitz, "Hawthorne and Spenser: Two Sources," *AL*, XXX (1958), 459-66; John W. Schroeder, "Hawthorne's 'Egotism; or, The Bosom Serpent,' and Its Source," *AL*, XXXI (1959), 150-62. For Bunyan see W. Stacy Johnson, "Hawthorne and *The Pilgrim's Progress*," *Journal of English and Germanic Philology*, L (1951), 156-66; Robert Stanton, "Hawthorne, Bunyan, and the American Romances," *PMLA*, LXXI (1956), 155-65.

5 Cf. Seymour L. Gross, "Hawthorne's 'My Kinsman, Major Molineux': History as Moral Adventure," *NCF*, XII (1957), 97-109.

6 Hawthorne's Gothicism has been elaborately, though not very profoundly, studied by Jane Lundblad, *Nathaniel Hawthorne and European Literary Tradition* (HUP, 1947). See also William Bysshe Stein, *Hawthorne's Faust: A Study of the Devil Archetype* (Fla, 1953) and N. F. Doubleday, "Hawthorne's Use of Three Gothic Patterns," *CE*, VII (1946), 250-62. On *Melmoth the Wanderer* see J. S. Goldstein, "The Literary Source of Hawthorne's *Fanshawe*," *MLN*, LX (1945), 1-8.

7 See Trollope's essay in appreciation, "The Genius of

Nathaniel Hawthorne," *North American Review*, CXXIX (1879), 203-22.

8   Robert L. Brant, "Hawthorne and Marvell," *AL*, XXX (1958), 366, suggests that the last sentence of *The Scarlet Letter* may come from Marvell's poem, "The Unfortunate Lover": "And he in Story only rules,/In a Field *Sable* a Lover *Gules*."

9   Vernon Loggins, op. cit. pp. 280-81, sees Rousseau's *Héloïse* as a source for *The Scarlet Letter*. Arlin Turner, "Hawthorne's Literary Borrowings," *PMLA*, LI (1936), 543-62, shows good reason to suppose that he was indebted to Madame de Staël's *Corinne* in both *Blithedale* and the *Faun*. Fannye N. Cherry, "The Source of Hawthorne's 'Young Goodman Brown,'" *AL*, V (1934), 342-8, suggests a story by Cervantes. See also J. Chesley Mathews, "Hawthorne's Knowledge of Dante," *UTSE*, 1940, pp. 157-65.

10   In an article called "Two Rodericks and Two Worms: 'Egotism; or, The Bosom Serpent' as Personal Satire," *PMLA*, LXXIV (1959), 607-12, Alfred H. Marks argues suggestively, though certainly not conclusively, that Roderick Ellison was intended to suggest Poe.

11   See Randall Stewart, "Hawthorne's Contributions to *The Salem Advertiser*," *AL*, V (1934), 327-41; Pat M. Ryan, Jr., "Young Hawthorne at the Salem Theatre," *EIHC*, XCIV (1958), 243-55.

12   Richard Mansfield had Joseph Hatton dramatize *The Scarlet Letter* for him in 1892, and the play did fail. But see Malcolm Cowley, "The Five Acts of *The Scarlet Letter*," *CE*, XIX (1951), 11-16, and Charles Ryskamp, "The New England Sources of *The Scarlet Letter*," *AL*, XXXI (1959), 257-72, which divides the novel into four acts, with a time-scheme. In 1926 the great Swedish director Victor Sjöström (or Seastrom, as they were calling him in this country), made a successful film of *The Scarlet Letter* for Metro-Goldwyn-Mayer, with Lillian Gish as Hester, Lars Hanson as Dimmesdale, and Henry B. Walthall as Chillingworth. Darrel Abel, "Hawthorne's Dimmesdale: Fugitive from Wrath," *NCF*, XI (1956), 81-105, says: "Hawthorne's narrative does not have the dramatic continuity of a moving picture; it has the static consecutiveness of a series of lantern slides, with interspersed commentary." There have been operas by Victor Damrosch (1896) and Vittorio Giannini (1938).

13   In his unpublished Ph.D. dissertation, "A Textual and Critical Edition of Hawthorne's *The Blithedale Romance*," University of Illinois, 1953; see also his article, " 'The Blithedale Romance' as Theatre," *NQ*, N.S. V (1958), 84-6.

14   "Hawthorne Amid the Alien Corn," *CE*, XVII (1956), 263-8. So far as I know, nobody has yet suggested that Hawthorne's novels are built like a ballet, but it is interesting to note the considerable dramatic use he makes of dancing, especially in *The Marble Faun*. (The association between opera and ballet and the habitual inclusion of a ballet in the older French opera should be remembered at this point.) See Norris Yates, "Ritual and Reality: Mask and Dance Motifs in Hawthorne's Fiction," *PQ*, XXXIV (1955), 56-70.

15   Leland Schubert, *Hawthorne as Artist: Fine-Art Devices in Fiction*, is vastly superior toward Hawthorne as an art critic and I think too much inclined to regard currently fashionable standards of evaluation as having been handed down from Sinai. It is all the more significant, then, that he should so justly appreciate Hawthorne's "intuitive" perception of painting. Hawthorne *"thinks* in terms of pictures, and makes impressive use of structure, design, rhythm, color, light-and-shade." Andrew Lang long ago compared Hawthorne's "effects of twilight-shades with a spot of glowing light and color" to the work of Rembrandt. For further interesting comment on these matters, see Walter Blair, "Color, Light, and Shadow in Hawthorne's Fiction," *NEQ*, XV (1942), 74-94, and Darrel Abel, "A Masque of Love and Death," *University of Toronto Quarterly*, XXIII (1953), 9-26.

16   Hawthorne's interest in the Venus de Medici is described in another connection on pp. 136-7.

17   In his unpublished Ph.D. dissertation, "The Personal Philosophy of Nathaniel Hawthorne," University of Florida, 1953.

18   See Hubert H. Hoeltje, "Hawthorne as a Senior at Bowdoin," *EIHC*, XCIV (1958), 205-28.

19   "When I was introduced to the President a few months ago I could perceive that he had never heard of me before." Extract from a letter to G. W. Curtis, 1862, in a fragment of a Goodspeed catalogue in the Longfellow House collection.

20   Bertha Faust, *Hawthorne's Contemporaneous Reputation* (University of Pennsylvania, 1939).

21 V. E. Gibbens, "Hawthorne's Note to 'Dr. Heidigger's Experiment,'" *MLN*, LX (1945), 408-9, points out that Hawthorne obviously did not read Dumas' *Memoires d'un medecin;* if he had done so, he would have perceived that the alleged resemblance between the two stories existed only in the imagination of the reviewer.

22 See letter to Robert Carter, from Concord, August 20, 1842, in the Berg Collection, New York Public Library.

23 In his study of the manuscript of *The Blithedale Romance* Dr. Crane has pointed out Hawthorne's tendency "to capitalize words referring to art, and especially to his own branch of art." In "Fancy's Show Box" he draws an analogy between plotting a story and plotting a deed. Writers who know that art is a form of living are not often inclined to think meanly of it. Walter de la Mare says that a poem is a deed. Both Scott and Joseph Conrad might have felt more comfortable about their work if they had been able to believe this.

24 James D. Rust, "George Eliot on *The Blithedale Romance*," *Boston Public Library Quarterly*, VII (1955), 207-15.

25 See pp. 112-15 of Randall Stewart's edition of *The American Notebooks*. This horrible experience haunted Hawthorne's imagination. Cf. *The Marble Faun*, Ch. XXV: "But speak the word, and it is like bringing up a drowned body out of the deepest pool of the rivulet, which has been aware of the horrible secret all along, in spite of its smiling surface."

26 For James, see Matthiessen, *American Renaissance*, and Marius Bewley, "James's Debt to Hawthorne," *Scrutiny*, XVI (1949), 178-95, 301-17; XVII (1950), 14-31; for Faulkner, William Van O'Connor "Hawthorne and Faulkner: Some Common Ground," *VQR*, XXXIII (1957), 105-23, and Randall Stewart, "Hawthorne and Faulkner," *CE*, XVII (1956), 258-62. Henry Seidel Canby's suggestion was made in *Classic Americans* (HB, 1931), Kenneth Cameron's in "Genesis of Hawthorne's 'The Ambitious Guest,'" *Historiographer of the Episcopal Diocese of Connecticut*, No. 14, Dec. 1955. The Lawrence references I owe to my pupil Miss Yvonne Romney, who points out that Donatello is like Paul in *Sons and Lovers*, when "he threw himself at full length on the turf, and pressed down his lips, kissing the violets and daisies," and that Donatello and Miriam behave like Mellors and Lady Chat-

terly, when "they pelted one another with early flowers; and gathering them up twined them with green leaves into garlands for their heads." In the chapter on Hawthorne in my *Cavalcade of the American Novel* (Holt, 1952), p. 47, I pointed out the resemblance between *The House of the Seven Gables*, Ch. XVII, and Section II of *To the Lighthouse*, by Virginia Woolf, and also that between Hawthorne's use of the organ-grinder in Ch. XVIII and Katherine Mansfield's in "The Daughters of the Late Colonel." I would add that "Wakefield" suggests both Melville and *The History of Mr. Polly*, by H. G. Wells.

27 Q. D. Leavis, "Hawthorne as Poet," *Sewanee Review*, LIX (1951), 179-205, 426-58, praises "the first great American novelists" for their determination "to find a non-naturalistic form for their work and to reject the English novelists' tradition of social comedy and melodrama, derived from the theater." She points out that, being a pioneer, Hawthorne tends to keep "close to the sources of literature." "His stage is the platform stage of early drama, his settings of the traditional sort such as are provided for by a tree, an archway, a street, a public square, a forest clearing, the outside of a church, a fountain or well or pool. His stage noticeably differs from his equally dramatic successor's—in comparison, James's is seen to be the modern three-sided box." The contrast between Hawthorne and James is interesting, but if the theater is to be equated with naturalism, which is doubtful at best, and if it represents what both James and Hawthorne are breaking away from, why does Mrs. Leavis find it necessary to describe their books in theatrical terms?

28 Darrel Abel illustrates the principles I have been trying to formulate with special application to *The House of the Seven Gables* in "Hawthorne's House of Tradition." *South Atlantic Quarterly*, LII (1953), 561-78. See also Jesse Bier, "Hawthorne on the Romance: His Prefaces Related and Examined," *Modern Philology*, LIII (1953), 17-24; Leon Howard, "Hawthorne's Fiction," *NCF*, VII (1953), 237-50; Ray B. Browne, "The Oft-Told Twice-Told Tales: Their Folklore Motifs," *Southern Folklore Quarterly*, XXII (1958), 69-83.

CHAPTER THREE: NATURE AND HUMANITY

1   See Henry G. Fairbanks, "Man's Separation from Nature: Hawthorne's Philosophy of Suffering and Death," *Christian Scholar*, XLII (1959), 51-63. "At most Hawthorne was a week-ender with nature."

2   Frank Davidson, "Hawthorne's Use of a Pattern from *The Rambler*," *MLN*, LXIII (1948), 545-8, shows how in some of the *Mosses* sketches, derived from Johnson, Hawthorne stresses "the indefiniteness and transiency of men's desires and their mistaken sense of values" instead of the "knavery" which Johnson had stressed. Alice L. Cooke, "Some Evidences of Hawthorne's Indebtedness to Swift," *UTSE*, 1938, pp. 140-62, makes a similar point about his use of materials derived from that writer.

3   For a succinct statement of the facts in the case, see Stewart, *Nathaniel Hawthorne*, pp. 87-9.

4   We owe the destruction of the legend of Madame Hawthorne primarily to the sound scholarship and common sense of her great-great-grandson, Manning Hawthorne. See his "Nathaniel Hawthorne Prepares for College," *EIHC*, XI (1938), 66-8; "A Glimpse of Hawthorne's Boyhood," *EIHC*, LXXXIII (1947), 178-84; and his review of Edward Mather's *Nathaniel Hawthorne, A Modest Man*, *NEQ*, XIV (1941), 386-91. Randall Stewart also puts the solitude of both Hawthorne and his mother into reasonable perspective in his biography.

5   Elizabeth L. Chandler, "Hawthorne's *Spectator*," *NEQ*, IV (1931), 289-330; Edward B. Hungerford, "Hawthorne Gossips About Salem," *NEQ*, VI (1933), 445-69.

6   For a fine consideration of some of the philosophical problems involved in Hawthorne's position, see James W. Mathews, "Hawthorne and the Chain of Being," *Modern Language Quarterly*, XVIII (1957), 282-94.

7   See N. F. Doubleday, "Hawthorne's Inferno," *CE*, I (1940), 658-70.

8   *Yesterdays with Authors*, pp. 52-3.

9   Manning Hawthorne, "Mary Louisa Hawthorne," *EIHC*, LXXV (1939), 103-34. See also his "Nathaniel Hawthorne at Bowdoin," *NEQ*, XIII (1940), 246-79.

10   I find it difficult to take seriously the story told by Edward W. Emerson, *Emerson in Concord* (HM, 1889), pp. 109-10, about Hawthorne looking at stereoptican views of Concord at the Emerson house and asking what they represented. We have endless testimony to the keenness of Hawthorne's observation. I cannot but think he was amusing himself or playing a game.

11   Louisa May Alcott was less generous in her estimate of the Hawthornes than her father. "Mr. H. is as queer as ever," she wrote to her cousin Ade May in Leicester, in an undated letter owned by Mrs. Margaret Parsons, of Worcester, Mass., "and we catch glimpses of a dark mysterious looking man in a big hat and red slippers darting over the hills or skimming by as if he expected the house of Alcott were about to rush out and clutch him. Mrs. H. is as sentimental and muffing as of old, wears crimson silk jackets, a rosary from Jerusalem, fire-flies in her hair and dirty white skirts with the sacred mud of London still extant thereon."

12   See Winfield S. Nevins, "Nathaniel Hawthorne's Removal from the Salem Custom House," *EIHC*, LIII (1917), 97-136.

13   D. K. Anderson, Jr., "Hawthorne's Crowds," *NCF*, VII (1952), 39-50.

14   Though there is no reason to suppose Hawthorne incapable of an oath upon occasion, it is not necessary to accept all the oaths which so unreliable a witness as Horace L. Conolly alone attributes to him. See Manning Hawthorne, "Hawthorne and 'The Man of God,' " *Colophon*, N.S. II (1937), 262-82. In *Septimius Felton* Hawthorne remarks that secluded men are likely to blaspheme when they are interrupted. Edward Dicey says he was disgusted when he heard a senator tell a broad story at a bar in Washington. "How would you like to see the Lord Chancellor of England making a fool of himself in a pot-house?"

15   Herbert Gorman attributed Judge Pyncheon's inferiority as a piece of characterization to the fact that Hawthorne was using him to pay off a score; he became "a rather stagy villain with a few Dickensian attributes," and "his pompous hypocrisy" was "emphasized to the detriment of reality." But Pyncheon is no more stagy than Hawthorne's other Gothic villains, none of whom shows him at his best. The most intemperate statement of the case against Hawthorne at the custom house is in a thoroughly subjective article

by Truman Nelson, "The Matrix of Place," *EIHC*, XCV (1959), 176-85.

16   Hubert H. Hoeltje, "Hawthorne as a Senior at Bowdoin," *EIHC*, XCIV (1958), 205-28.

17   Lewis Mumford's suggestion, *Herman Melville* (HB, 1929), that Hawthorne caricatured Melville in "Ethan Brand" is one of the worst *gaffes* in twentieth-century criticism: the story was written and published before the two ever met. See Randall Stewart, "Ethan Brand," *Saturday Review of Literature*, V (1929), 968; E. K. Brown, "Hawthorne, Melville, and 'Ethan Brand,' " *AL*, III (1931), 72-5. See also Edward G. Lueders, "The Melville-Hawthorne Relationship in *Pierre* and *The Blithedale Romance*," *Western Humanities Review*, IV (1950), 323-34.

18   The frankness of Hawthorne's comments on Cilley in *The American Notebooks* (see Randall Stewart's edition, p. 286) were toned down when he published his sketch of him. Julian Hawthorne, *Nathaniel Hawthorne and His Wife*, I, 173-5, suggested that Hawthorne felt guilt for Cilley's death in a duel because he himself had nearly set him the example of fighting one. See Hawthorne's letter to Bridge and Stewart's comment on it, in *American Notebooks*, p. 286. The tissue of speculation which Robert Cantwell weaves about the matter in his *Nathaniel Hawthorne: The American Years*, pp. 229-31, is, like most of the speculations in that otherwise useful work, absurd.

CHAPTER FOUR: THE CITIZEN

1   The fullest account of the subject indicated is in Royal Cortissoz' unpublished Ph.D. dissertation, "The Political Life of Nathaniel Hawthorne," New York University, 1955. See, also, Henry G. Fairbanks, "Citizen Hawthorne and the Perennial Problems of American Society," *Revue de l'Université d'Ottawa*, XXIX (1959), 26-38.

2   See N. F. Doubleday, "Hawthorne's Criticism of New England Life," *CE*, II (1941), 639-53.

3   For Harry Levin, see his book *The Power of Blackness: Hawthorne; Poe; Melville* (Knopf, 1958). This was an important element in the age's thinking. Longfellow expressed it in "A Psalm of Life," having learned it from Goethe and a German inscription:

Blicke nicht trauernd in die Vergangenheit,
sie kommt nicht wieder; nütze weise die Gegenwart,
sie ist dein; der düstern Zukunft geh ohne
Furcht mit männlichen Sinne entgegen.

4 For a full account of Hawthorne's labors in behalf of maritime reform, see Laurence S. Hall, *Hawthorne, Critic of Society*, Ch. I.

5 See James E. Miller, Jr., "Hawthorne and Melville: The Unpardonable Sin," *PMLA*, LXX (1955), 91-114.

6 Darrel Abel, "Hawthorne's Skepticism About Social Reform," *UKCR*, XIX (1953), 181-93, and compare N. F. Doubleday, "Hawthorne's Satirical Allegory," *CE*, III (1941), 325-37; Arlin Turner, "Hawthorne and Reform," *NEQ*, XV (1942), 700-714; Russell Kirk, "The Moral Conservatism of Hawthorne," *Contemporary Review*, CLXXXII (1952), 361-6.

7 The following letter about this matter to a "Mr. Woodman" (Concord, June 22, 1862) is in the Morgan Library:

I am sorry I misquoted Emerson. I never saw the speech or article in which the phrase appeared, and know no more of it than that single sentence, which reached me in England. Your version of it certainly makes a considerable difference, as allowing the reader or auditor (if he pleases) to put John Brown at a somewhat lower elevation than Jesus Christ. But, as a mere matter of taste, surely it had better never have been said. If Emerson chooses to plant John Brown's gallows on Mount Calvary, the moral and religious sense of mankind will insist on its being placed between the crosses of the two thieves, and not side by side with that of the Savior. I wish he would not say such things, and deem him less excusable than other men; for his apophthegms (though they often have strange life in them) do not so burn and sting his mouth that he is compelled to drop them out of it.

Chapter Five: THE FIRE IN THE MEMBERS

1 See Bliss Perry, "Hawthorne at North Adams," in *The Amateur Spirit* (HM, 1905).

2 Stewart, *Nathaniel Hawthorne: A Biography*, p. 43.

3 See Norman Holmes Pearson, "Hawthorne's Duel," *EIHC*, XCIV (1958), 229-42, where the identifications were finally made.

4 See Louis A. Haselmayer, "Hawthorne and the Cenci,"

Neophilologus, XXVII (1927), 59-65; Nathalia Wright, "Hawthorne and the Praslin Murder," *NEQ*, XV (1942), 5-14; and cf. Edward Wagenknecht, *Cavalcade of the American Novel*, p. 49, n. 23.

5 According to Leonard J. Fick, *The Light Beyond: A Study of Hawthorne's Theology* (Newman Press, 1955), when Hester and Dimmesdale agreed to go away together he "yielded himself . . . to what he knew was deadly sin." But Hester was confused. "In the terminology of the theologians, therefore, Dimmesdale committed a formal sin. Hester committed a material sin—and a material sin brings neither guilt nor stain to the soul. In the sight of God she committed no sin at all, always assuming, of course, that her ignorance of the law was inculpable."

6 See Matthiessen, *American Renaissance*, p. 297, n. 5.

7 Darrel Abel, "Hawthorne's Skepticism About Social Reform," *UKCR*, XIX (1953), 181-93.

8 Hilda has been excoriated by critics times without number, never more mercilessly than by Professor Waggoner, who dedicates almost five pages of his *Hawthorne: A Critical Study* (202-7) to her destruction. She is "a lifeless convention lifted bodily from the nineteenth-century romances and the steel engravings of the Christmas gift books"; she is "Mark Twain's conception of Olivia and Hawthorne's of Sophia." She is "completely unbelieveable," and "if she can be judged in moral terms at all, she must be considered guilty of a pharisaical form of spiritual pride." We cannot save her even by reading her as "Spirit," for this would make Spirit "look very unattractive and even immoral, inferior indeed in grace to the human world." "Throughout most of the story she rejects the world because it is sinful while she is perfectly pure." There is no denying that Hilda fails Miriam when Miriam needs her most, but it will not do to ignore the fact that she is bleeding and in danger of death from her own wound—the merciless, blinding revelation of evil, which, through no fault of her own, was thrust upon her at the Tarpeian Rock. She is in no condition to help anybody; instead she herself stands in desperate need of help! Is Professor Waggoner sure that she "rejects the world because it is sinful while she is perfectly pure"? That the world is sinful is not debatable, but may it not be that Hilda "rejects" it in humility rather than in sinful pride, recognizing her own weakness and struggling not to

betray her own citadel? May there not even be a touch of pride in Professor Waggoner's own assumption that he understands Olivia Clemens and Sophia Hawthorne better than their husbands did? He also ignores the continued vogue of the Hilda-type of heroine in popular art clear down to the vogue of the "flapper" and her successors—and beyond.

9 See W. Stacy Johnson, "Sin and Salvation in Hawthorne," *Hibbert Journal*, L (1951), 39-47.

10 See N. H. Pearson's Ph.D. dissertation, "The French and Italian Notebooks of Nathaniel Hawthorne," II, 727.

11 Julian Hawthorne gave the date of his mother's birth as September 21, 1811 but this was clearly an error for 1809. See Robert Cantwell, op. cit., p. 238, and Louise Hall Tharp, *The Peabody Sisters of Salem* (LB, 1950), p. 342. Mrs. Tharp's book, one of the most charming of recent biographical works about the nineteenth century, covers the lives of Mrs. Hawthorne and both her sisters.

12 Manning Hawthorne, "Aunt Ebe: Some Letters of Elizabeth M. Hawthorne," *NEQ*, XX (1947), 209-31; see also his "Mary Louisa Hawthorne," *EIHC*, LXXV (1939), 103-34.

13 See Randall Stewart, "Letters to Sophia," *Huntington Library Quarterly*, VI (1944), 387-95.

14 Louise Hall Tharp, op. cit., p. 158.

15 N. H. Pearson, "Elizabeth Peabody on Hawthorne," *EIHC*, XCIV (1958), 256-76. The reader who glances at the birth-dates of the Hawthorne children in Chapter I of this book will see that "planned parenthood" could hardly have been more carefully worked out. There was one miscarriage, however; see Stewart, *American Notebooks*, p. 173.

16 The picturesque story about the beginning of *The Scarlet Letter*—how when Hawthorne came home in despair to tell Sophia he had lost his position in the custom house, she delightedly exclaimed, "Oh, then you can write your book!" and when he inquired what they were to live on while he was writing it, she triumphantly brought out the money she had saved—cannot be literally true. The dismissal did not come as a surprise, and the exact time when Hawthorne began work on the novel is not known. See Hubert H. Hoeltje, "The Writing of *The Scarlet Letter*," *NEQ*, XXVII (1954), 326-46.

CHAPTER SIX: GOD'S CHILD

1 There is an 1848 reference to Una having gone, on her own fiat, to "Dr. Flint's church" in Salem.

2 There is a systematic consideration of most of the topics considered in this chapter in an unpublished Ph.D. dissertation by George W. Bowman, "Hawthorne and Religion" (Indiana University, 1954).

3 Neal F. Doubleday, "The Theme of Hawthorne's 'Fancy's Show Box,'" *AL*, X (1938), 341-3.

4 Tremaine McDowell, "Nathaniel Hawthorne and the Witches of Colonial Salem," *NQ*, CLXVI (1934), 152, points out that Goody Cloyse, Goody Cory, and Martha Carrier, all specifically mentioned in "Young Goodman Brown" were sentenced to death by Judge John Hathorne in 1692. This narrative, probably Hawthorne's greatest short story, might be considered an exception to his consistency in portraying witchcraft as a delusion. It is true that he employs his usual ambivalent technique in this tale, forcing the reader himself to choose between Brown's having experienced or only dreamed (or imagined) the things he saw in the forest. Since the subject of the tale was Brown's own loss of faith in life and in mankind as the result of his night in the forest there were sound aesthetic reasons why the story should have been handled in this way. Generally Hawthorne manages to load his scales in behalf of the supernatural when offering a choice between natural and supernatural (see n. 11); here I think we may say he loads them on the other side. Young Goodman Brown goes to the forest with hell in his heart; he finds what he expected to find, as men always do. " 'There,' resumed the sable form, 'are *all* whom ye have reverenced from youth'" (italics mine). Hawthorne could not possibly have been cynical enough to regard this as a statement of fact or desire to have the reader so accept it. (Since writing this note I have come across three recent articles on "Young Goodman Brown," all worthy of attention: Thomas F. Walsh, Jr., "The Bedeviling of Young Goodman Brown," *Modern Language Quarterly*, XIX [1958], 331-6; Joseph T. McCullen, "Young Goodman Brown: Presumption and Despair," *Discourse*, II [1959], 145-57; Paul W. Miller, "Hawthorne's 'Young Goodman Brown': Cynicism or Meliorism?" *NCF*, XIV [1959], 255-64.)

5 Seymour L. Gross, "Hawthorne's Revision of 'The Gentle Boy,'" *AL*, XXVI (1954), 196-208, shows how the final version of the story dropped apologies or explanations for Puritan behavior which had been included when the story appeared in *The Token*. In his excellent unpublished Ph.D. dissertation, " 'Eternal Truth': A Study of Nathaniel Hawthorne's Philosophy" (Indiana University, 1950), B. Bernard Cohen points out that even Tobias Pearson fails to win Hawthorne's full approval. "He is essentially a weak character; ultimately he... [leaves the Puritans] and becomes a fanatical Quaker. It is his wife who represents the balanced individual in the story."

6 Joseph Schwartz, "A Note on Hawthorne's Fatalism," *MLN*, LXX (1955), 33-6.

7 Arlin Turner, "A Note on Hawthorne's Revisions," *MLN*, LI (1936), 426-9.

8 "Nathaniel Hawthorne," in Harold C. Gardiner, ed., *American Classics Reconsidered* (Scribners, 1958). See also Marvin Fisher, "Johnson and Hawthorne's Conservatism," *Journal of the History of Ideas*, XIX (1958), 173-96.

9 See Chapter V, n. 5.

10 Stewart, *Nathaniel Hawthorne*, p. 98. On the general matter discussed in this paragraph see G. P. Voight, "Hawthorne and the Roman Catholic Church," *NEQ*, XIX (1946), 394-7, and three articles by Henry G. Fairbanks, "Hawthorne and the Catholic Church," *BUSE*, I (1955), 148-65, "Hawthorne and Confession," *Catholic Historical Review*, XLIII (1957), 38-45, and "Hawthorne and the Nature of Man: Changing Personality Concepts in the Nineteenth Century," *Revue de l'Université d'Ottawa*, XXVIII (1958), 309-22. Theodore Maynard's curious impression that Hawthorne had a bad conscience toward the Catholic Church is absurd; he has been rebuked for it by at least one Catholic scholar.

11 In her unpublished Ph.D. dissertation, "Hawthorne and the Supernatural" (Stanford University, 1937), Miss Evelyn C. Johnson found no evidence "to prove that Hawthorne believed in any visible connection with . . . [the] world of spirits. Hawthorne was not a mystic; there was too much skepticism and realism in his nature to make him one." She drew the conclusion that "he uses the supernatural . . . primarily as a literary device. The supernatural supplied the 'marvellous' element which he considered important

in the creation of a romance." But Hawthorne did not create in the spirit of Poe's "The Philosophy of Composition." Though he generally gives the reader his choice between natural and super-natural explanations of the phenomena under consideration, it is clear in most cases that he does not intend him to choose the natural explanation for the simple reason that the story will become point-less and uninteresting if he does. In offering a choice Hawthorne concedes to the skepticism of the age including his own share of it. But doubt has reinforced the appeal of the supernatural in liter-ature from time immemorial, and in life too, and doubt adds mean-ing to religion as death adds meaning to life. Hawthorne was the last man to force a belief upon anybody. The reader must choose. and judge himself by his choice.

12   "Try—some evening when you are alone and happy, and when you are most conscious of loving me and of being loved by me—and see if you do not possess this power already." And again: "I *was* conscious, on those two evenings, of a peacefulness and contented repose such as I never enjoyed before. You could not have felt such quiet unless I had felt it too—nor could I, unless you had."

13   In "The Ghost of Dr. Harris," *Works*, "Old Manse Edi-tion," XVI, 244-54.

14   Miss Shepard mediated between "spirits" and various members of the circle. Mrs. Hawthorne received comforting mes-sages from her recently deceased mother. But the most remarkable communications came from a boisterous spirit who called herself Mary Runnel or Rondel and who claimed the sympathy of Nathan-iel Hawthorne on the ground of a prior connection with his family. The name was unknown to Hawthorne but after his death Julian discovered that in the 1750's there had been an abortive love affair between Daniel Hathorne and a girl thus named. See "Old Manse Edition," XXI, 198, and three works by Julian Hawthorne: *Nathaniel Hawthorne and His Wife*, I, 31-5; *The Memoirs of Julian Hawthorne* (M, 1938), pp. 205-8; *Hawthorne Reading*, p. 50. Hosmer, "Science and Pseudo-Science," p. 300, n. 68, seems to have a variant version of this story. For the general subject, see Kather-ine H. Porter, *Through a Glass Darkly: Spiritualism in the Brown-ing Circle* (University of Kansas Press, 1958).

15 "The Hollow of the Three Hills" (1830) is interesting in connection with Hawthorne's attitude toward spiritualism. The entire story is devoted to the description of a séance. The "withered hag" who acts as medium harms no one, yet Hawthorne says that she poured forth "the monotonous words of a prayer that was not meant to be acceptable in heaven." He gives no explanation of why he thinks of her as having done wrong.

16 Bliss Perry, *Park Street Papers* (HM, 1908), pp. 102-3.

17 For fuller discussion of these matters, see Cohen, " 'Eternal Truth' "; Fick, *The Light Within;* Barriss Millis, "Hawthorne and Puritanism," *NEQ,* XXI (1948), 78-102; and two articles by Darrel Abel: "Hawthorne's Pearl: Symbol and Character," *ELH,* XVIII (1951), 50-66, and "The Devil in Boston," *PQ,* XXXII (1953), 366-81.

18 As Fick points out, in Christian theology the only unpardonable sin is "the sin of final impenitence." If the sinner refuses to turn from his sins and seek forgiveness for them, he renders God's Infinite Mercy inoperative in its relation to himself. Hawthorne uses the term with reference to those sins which so harden the heart that forgiveness becomes unlikely or impossible. See, further, James E. Miller, Jr. (see Ch. 4, n. 5); Joseph X. Brennan and Seymour L. Gross, "The Origin of Hawthorne's Unpardonable Sin," *BUSE,* III (1957), 123-9; and, from a very different point of view, Barry A. Marks, "The Origin of Original Sin in Hawthorne's Fiction," *NCF,* XIV (1960), 359-62, a suggestive treatment of Hawthorne's ambivalence on the special subject of guilt and moral responsibility.

19 George Edward Woodberry (*Nathaniel Hawthorne*) exaggerates Hawthorne's implacability and fails to discern the Christian elements in his thinking. Woodberry calls Miriam and Donatello's sense of union with sinners "a curious inversion of the communion of the saints" and seems to think of it as something peculiar to Puritanism. It is not, for St. Paul expresses it in the Epistle to the Romans.

20 "Suggestions for Interpreting The Marble Faun," *AL,* XIII (1941), 224-39. For other discussions of the matter, from various points of view, see Donald A. Ringe, "Hawthorne's Psychology of the Head and Heart," *PMLA,* LXV (1950), 120-32; Merle E. Brown, "The Structure of *The Marble Faun,*" *AL,*

XXVIII (1956), 302-13; Henry G. Fairbanks, "Sin, Free Will, and 'Pessimism' in Hawthorne," *PMLA*, LXXI (1956), 975-89; Bernard J. Paris, "Optimism and Pessimism in *The Marble Faun*," *BUSE*, II (1956), 95-112. F. O. Matthiessen (*American Renaissance*, pp. 311-12) usefully pointed out that we do not need Hilda's anguished denial of Miriam's position—made "during the Roman Carnival, with its vestiges of the old pagan rite of spring"—to know where Hawthorne stands. The whole tenor of the book contradicts Miriam: she spends the rest of her life in penitence, Donatello his in prison. For John Erskine's article see "The Theme of Death in *Paradise Lost*," *PMLA*, XXXII (1917), 573-82. Arthur O. Lovejoy's reply, "Milton and the Paradox of the Fortunate Fall," *ELH*, IV (1937), includes references to the other important replies.

21 In his *American Literature and Christian Doctrine* (LSUP, 1958).

22 Darrel Abel, "Hawthorne's Hester," *CE*, XIII (1952), 303-9, wisely says that Hester "typifies Romantic individualism, and in her story Hawthorne endeavored to exhibit the inadequacy of such a philosophy." It is clear, I think, that she does repent and achieve her reconciliation in the last chapter, where she returns to Boston voluntarily—"here had been her sin [no "consecration" now!]; here her sorrow; and here was to be her penitence"—and voluntarily picks up the scarlet letter which before had been imposed upon her. In its former aspect it had driven her into heresy; now it heals. Hawthorne has not traced the process of her later development, but he has not recorded how she fell into sin either. Dimmesdale is followed to the end, but we see Hester's development in detail only in one portion of her career.

23 "The Questionable Shapes of Nathaniel Hawthorne," *Living Age*, CCXLII (1904), 348-53.

24 *Hawthorne: A Critical Study*, pp. 229ff.

SOME BOOKS
ABOUT HAWTHORNE

Hawthorne bibliography is plethoric, and in view of the excellent listings elsewhere available I have not thought it advisable to take the space for another extensive listing here. The reader is referred to Robert E. Spiller et al., eds., *Literary History of the United States* (M, 1948), III, 544-53, and the *Bibliography Supplement*, edited by Richard M. Ludwig (M, 1959), pp. 133-6; to Austin Warren, ed., *Nathaniel Hawthorne: Representative Selections* (ABC, 1934); to Lewis Leary, *Articles on American Literature, 1900-1950* (Duke, 1954); and to my own *Cavalcade of the American Novel* (Holt, 1952).

Many books and dissertations dealing with specialized subjects, as well as a great many articles, are mentioned in the Notes immediately preceding this section. Sometimes these works are cited as authorities; more often I am attempting to guide the reader to further information on the subject. For a list of the abbreviations employed, both here and in the notes themselves, see p. 203.

The most desirable editions of Hawthorne are the limited "Autograph Edition," 22 volumes (HM, 1900) and the "Old Manse Edition" (1904), printed from the same plates. Hawthorne's notebooks appear in these sets as bowdlerized by Mrs. Hawthorne; accurate texts are available in Randall Stewart's editions of *The American Notebooks* (YUP, 1932) and *The English Notebooks* (Modern Language Association, 1941). All earlier editions of *Dr. Grimshawe's Secret* have now been superseded by the one edited by Edward H. Davidson (HUP, 1954); see also his *Hawthorne's Last Phase* (YUP, 1949). Hawthorne's contributions to *The American Magazine of Useful and Entertaining Knowledge* have been reprinted by Arlin Turner, *Hawthorne as Editor* (LSUP, 1941). Opinion is divided concerning the authenticity of Samuel T. Pickard, ed., *Hawthorne's First Diary* (HM, 1897).

The basic biographical study is Julian Hawthorne, *Nathaniel Hawthorne and His Wife*, 2 vols. (HM, 1884); see also his *Hawthorne and His Circle* (H, 1903). Both *Nathaniel Hawthorne and His Wife* and Rose Hawthorne Lathrop, *Memories of Hawthorne* (HM, 1897) contain many letters. There are two collections of letters in two volumes each: *Love Letters of Nathaniel Hawthorne* (Chicago, Society of the Dofobs, 1907) and *Letters of Hawthorne to William D. Ticknor, 1851-1864* (Newark, The Carteret Book Club, 1910). Many of the letters in this second collection also appear in Caroline Ticknor, *Hawthorne and His Publisher* (HM, 1913). See also the Hawthorne section in James C. Austin, *Fields of The Atlantic Monthly* (Huntington Library, 1953).

An extensive Hawthorne bibliography by Nouvart Tasjian and D. Eckerman, long promised, seems destined to join Norman H. Pearson's edition of the "French and Italian Notebooks" and his collection of Hawthorne's letters as the most famous unpublished books in American literature. Less ambitious bibliographies are Nina C. Browne, *A Bibliography of Nathaniel Hawthorne* (HM, 1905) and Wallace C. Cathcart, *Bibliography of the Works of Nathaniel Hawthorne* (Cleveland, Rowfant Club, 1905). See also John D. Gordan, *Nathaniel Hawthorne: The Years of Fulfilment, 1804-1853: An Exhibition from the Berg Collection, First Editions, Manuscripts, Autograph Letters* (New York Public Library, 1954).

The best modern biography of Hawthorne is Randall Stewart, *Nathaniel Hawthorne: A Biography* (YUP, 1948). Robert Cantwell, *Nathaniel Hawthorne: The American Years* (Rinehart, 1948) brings much interesting material together but the author has a weakness for fantastic hypotheses. Mark Van Doren, *Nathaniel Hawthorne* (Sloane, 1949) is an excellent biographical-critical study.

The best of the older books about Hawthorne are George P. Lathrop, *A Study of Hawthorne* (HM, 1876); George Edward Woodberry, *Nathaniel Hawthorne* (HM, 1902); F. P. Stearns, *The Life and Genius of Nathaniel Hawthorne* (LG, 1906). First-hand data are preserved in Horatio Bridge, *Personal Recollections of Nathaniel Hawthorne* (H, 1893) and F. B. Sanborn, *Hawthorne and His Friends* (Torch Press, 1908). See also James T. Fields,

Yesterdays with Authors (HM, 1872). W. C. Brownell's essay in *American Prose Masters* (S, 1909) is brilliant, unsympathetic, and opinionated.

Lloyd Morris, *The Rebellious Puritan* (HB, 1927); Herbert Gorman, *Hawthorne: A Study in Solitude* (D, 1927); and Newton Arvin, *Hawthorne* (LB, 1929) reflect biographical methods in vogue during the 'twenties. Edward Mather, *Nathaniel Hawthorne, A Modest Man* (Crowell, 1940) added little. The best modern account of Hawthorne in book form before Stewart was the Hawthorne section in F. O. Matthiessen, *American Renaissance* (Oxford University Press, 1941), still a brilliant study.

In *The Yellow Ruff and* The Scarlet Letter (Fla, 1955), Alfred S. Reid argued that the novel was based on the murder of Sir Thomas Overbury (which Hawthorne himself mentions). But most recent Hawthorne books have been critical rather than biographical, and a number of them apply "new critical" methods. The following are all useful in whole or in part: Leland Schubert: *Hawthorne the Artist: Fine-Art Devices in Fiction* (University of North Carolina Press, 1944); Richard Harter Fogle, *Hawthorne's Fiction: The Light and the Dark* (Okla, 1952); Hyatt H. Waggoner, *Hawthorne: A Critical Study* (HUP, 1955); Roy R. Male, *Hawthorne's Tragic Vision* (University of Texas Press, 1957).

INDEX